HANDBOOK OF NATURE-STUDY:

INTRODUCTIONS TO NATURE-STUDY

COMPLETE YOUR COLLECTION TODAY!

HANDBOOK OF NATURE-STUDY

Reptiles, Amphibians, Fish and Invertebrates

HANDBOOK OF NATURE-STUDY

Birds

HANDBOOK OF NATURE-STUDY

Wildflowers, Weeds and Cultivated Crops

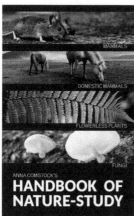

HANDBOOK OF NATURE-STUDY

Mammals and Flowerless Plants

HANDBOOK OF NATURE-STUDY

Trees and Garden Flowers

HANDBOOK OF NATURE-STUDY

Earth and Sky

HANDBOOK OF NATURE-STUDY

Insects

HANDBOOK OF NATURE-STUDY

Introduction

Handbook of Nature-Study:

Introductions to Nature-Study

ANNA BOTSFORD COMSTOCK, B.S., L.H.D

LATE PROFESSOR OF NATURE-STUDY IN CORNELL UNIVERSITY

LIVING BOOK
PRESS

This edition published 2020
by Living Book Press

ISBN: 978-1-922348-75-3 (hardcover)
        978-1-922348-74-6 (softcover)

 A catalogue record for this book is available from the National Library of Australia

THE TEACHING OF NATURE-STUDY

THE TEACHING OF NATURE-STUDY

WHAT NATURE-STUDY IS

NATURE-STUDY is, despite all discussions and perversions, a study of nature; it consists of simple, truthful observations that may, like beads on a string, finally be threaded upon the understanding and thus held together as a logical and harmonious whole. Therefore, the object of the nature-study teacher should be to cultivate in the children powers of accurate observation and to build up within them, understanding.

WHAT NATURE-STUDY SHOULD DO FOR THE CHILD

FIRST, but not most important, nature-study gives the child practical and helpful knowledge. It makes him familiar with nature's ways and forces, so that he is not so helpless in the presence of natural misfortune and disasters.

Nature-study cultivates the child's imagination since there are so many wonderful and true stories that he may read with his own eyes, which affect his imagination as much as does fairy lore; at the

1

same time nature-study cultivates in him a perception and a regard for what *is* true, and the power to express it. All things seem possible in nature; yet this seeming is always guarded by the eager quest of what is true. Perhaps, half the falsehood in the world is due to lack of power to detect the truth and to express it. Nature-study aids both in discernment and expression of things as they are.

Nature-study cultivates in the child a love of the beautiful; it brings to him early a perception of color, form and music. He sees whatever there is in his environment, whether it be the thunder-head piled up in the western sky, or the golden flash of the oriole in the elm; whether it be the purple of the shadows on the snow, or the azure glint on the wing of the little butterfly. Also, what there is of sound, he hears; he reads the music score of the bird orchestra, separating each part and knowing which bird sings it. And the patter of the rain, the gurgle of the brook, the sighing of the wind in the pine, he notes and loves and becomes enriched thereby.

But, more than all, nature-study gives the child a sense of companionship with life out of doors and an abiding love of nature. Let this latter be the teacher's criterion for judging his or her work. If nature-study as taught does not make the child love nature and the out-

of-doors, then it should cease. Let us not inflict permanent injury on the child by turning him away from nature instead of toward it. However, if the love of nature is in the teacher's heart, there is no danger; such a teacher, no matter by what method, takes the child gently by the hand and walks with him in paths that lead to the seeing and comprehending of what he may find beneath his feet or above his head. And these paths whether they lead among the lowliest plants, or whether to the stars, finally converge and bring the wanderer to that serene peace and hopeful faith that is the sure inheritance of all those who realize fully that they are working units of this wonderful universe.

NATURE-STUDY AS A HELP TO HEALTH

PERHAPS the most valuable practical lesson the child gets from nature-study is a personal knowledge that nature's laws are not to be evaded. Wherever he looks, he discovers that attempts at such evasion result in suffering and death. A knowledge thus naturally attained of the immutability of nature's "must" and "shall not" is in itself a moral education. That the fool as well as the transgressor fares ill in breaking natural laws, makes for wisdom in morals as well as in hygiene.

Out-of-door life takes the child afield and keeps him in the open air, which not only helps him physically and occupies his mind with sane subjects, but keeps him out of mischief. It is not only during childhood that this is true, for love of nature counts much for sanity in later life. This is an age of nerve tension, and the relaxation which comes from the comforting companionship found in woods and fields is, without doubt, the best remedy for this condition. Too many men who seek the out-of-doors for rest at the present time, can only find it with a gun in hand. To rest and heal their nerves they must go out and try to kill some unfortunate creature,—the old, old story of sacrificial blood. Far better will it be when, through properly training the child, the man shall be enabled to enjoy nature through seeing how creatures live rather than watching them die. It is the sacred privilege of nature-study to do this for future generations and for him thus trained, shall the words of Longfellow's poem to Agassiz apply:

"And he wandered away and away, with Nature the dear old nurse,
Who sang to him night and day, the rhymes of the universe.
And when the way seemed long, and his heart began to fail,
She sang a more wonderful song, or told a more wonderful tale."

WHAT NATURE-STUDY SHOULD DO FOR THE TEACHER

DURING many years, I have been watching teachers in our public schools in their conscientious and ceaseless work; and so far as I can foretell, the fate that awaits them finally is either nerve exhaustion or nerve atrophy. The teacher must become either a neurasthenic or a "clam."

I have had conversations with hundreds of teachers in the public schools of New York State concerning the introduction of nature-study into the curriculum, and most of them declared, "Oh, we have not time for it. Every moment is full now!" Their nerves were at such a tension that with one more thing to do they must fall apart. The question in my own mind during these conversations was always, how long can she stand it! I asked some of them, "Did you ever try a vigorous walk in the open air in the open country every Saturday or every Sunday of your teaching year?" "Oh no!" they exclaimed in despair of making me understand. "On Sunday we must go to church or see our friends and on Saturday we must do our shopping or our sewing. We must go to the dressmaker's lest we go unclad, we must mend, and darn stockings; we need Saturday to catch up."

Yes, catch up with more cares, more worries, more fatigue, but not with more growth, more strength, more vigor and more courage for work. In my belief, there are two and only two occupations for Saturday afternoon or forenoon for a teacher. One is to be out of doors and the other is to lie in bed, and the first is best. Out in this, God's beautiful world, there is everything waiting to heal lacerated nerves, to strengthen tired muscles, to please and content the soul that is torn to shreds with duty and care. To the teacher who turns to nature's healing, nature-study in the schoolroom is not a trouble; it is a sweet, fresh breath of air blown across the heat of radiators and the noisome odor of over-crowded small humanity. She, who opens her eyes and her heart nature-ward even once a week, finds nature-study in the schoolroom a delight and an abiding joy. What does such a one find in her schoolroom instead of the terrors of discipline, the eternal watching and eternal nagging to keep the pupils quiet and at work? She finds, first of all, companionship with her children; and second, she finds that without planning or going on a far voyage, she has found health and strength.

WHEN AND WHY THE TEACHER SHOULD SAY "I DO NOT KNOW"

NO SCIENCE professor in any university, if he be a man of high attainment, hesitates to say to his pupils, "I do not know," if they ask for information beyond his knowledge. The greater his scientific reputation and erudition, the more readily, simply and without apology he says this. He, better than others, comprehends how vast is the region that lies beyond man's present knowledge. It is only the teacher in the elementary schools who has never received enough scientific training to reveal to her how little she does know, who feels that she must appear to know everything or her pupils will lose confidence in her. But how useless is this pretence, in nature-study! The pupils, whose younger eyes are much keener for details than hers, will soon discover her limitations and then their distrust of her will be real.

In nature-study any teacher can with honor say, "I do not know;" for perhaps, the question asked is as yet unanswered by the great scientists. But she should not let her lack of knowledge be a wet blanket thrown over her pupils' interest. She should say frankly, "I do not know; let us see if we cannot together find out this mysterious thing. Maybe no one knows it as yet, and I wonder if you will discover it before I do." She thus conveys the right impression, that only a little about the intricate life of plants and animals is yet known; and at the same time she makes her pupils feel the thrill and zest of investigation. Nor will she lose their respect by doing this, if she does it in the right spirit. For three years, I had for comrades in my walks afield, two little children and they kept me busy saying, "I do not know." But they never lost confidence in me or in my knowledge; they simply gained respect for the vastness of the unknown.

The chief charm of nature-study would be taken away if it did not lead us through the border-land of knowledge into the realm of the undiscovered. Moreover, the teacher, in confessing her ignorance and at the same time her interest in a subject, establishes between herself and her pupils a sense of

Shishirdasika (cc by-sa 4.0)
Spurred Butterfly Pea

5

companionship which relieves the strain of discipline, and gives her a new and intimate relation with her pupils which will surely prove a potent element in her success. The best teacher is always one who is the good comrade of her pupils.

NATURE-STUDY, THE ELIXIR OF YOUTH

THE old teacher is too likely to become didactic, dogmatic and "bossy" if she does not constantly strive with herself. Why? She has to be thus five days in the week and, therefore, she is likely to be so seven. She knows arithmetic, grammar and geography to their uttermost and she is never allowed to forget that she knows them, and finally her interests become limited to what she knows.

After all, what is the chief sign of growing old? Is it not the feeling that we know all there is to be known? It is not years which make people old; it is ruts, and a limitation of interests. When we no longer care about anything except our own interests, we are then old, it matters not whether our years be twenty or eighty. It is rejuvenation for the teacher, thus growing old, to stand ignorant as a child in the presence of one of the simplest of nature's miracles—the formation of a crystal, the evolution of the butterfly from the caterpillar, the exquisite adjustment of the silken lines in the spider's orb-web. I know how to "make magic" for the teacher who is growing old. Let her go out with her youngest pupil and fall on her knees before the miracle of the blossoming violet and say: "Dear Nature, I know naught of the wondrous life of these, your smallest creatures. Teach me!" and she will suddenly find herself young.

NATURE STUDY AS A HELP IN SCHOOL DISCIPLINE

MUCH of the naughtiness in school is a result of the child's lack of interest in his work, augmented by the physical inaction that results from an attempt to sit quietly. The best teachers try to obviate both of these rather than to punish because of them. Nature-study is an aid in both respects, since it keeps the child interested and also gives him something to do.

In the nearest approach to an ideal school that I have ever seen, for children of second grade, the pupils were allowed, as a reward of merit, to visit the aquaria or the terrarium for periods of five minutes, which time was given to the blissful observation of the fascinating prisoners. The teacher also allowed the reading of stories about the plants and animals under observation to be regarded as a reward of merit. As I entered the schoolroom, there were eight or ten of the children at the windows watching eagerly what was happening to the creatures confined there in the various cages. There was a mud aquarium for the frogs and salamanders, an aquarium for fish, many small aquaria for insects and each had one or two absorbingly interested spectators who were quiet, well behaved and were getting their nature-study lessons in an ideal manner. The teacher told me that the problem of discipline was solved by this method, and that she was rarely obliged to rebuke or punish. In many other schools, watching the living creatures in the aquaria, or terrarium has been used as a reward for other work well done.

THE RELATION OF NATURE-STUDY TO SCIENCE

NATURE-STUDY is not elementary science as so taught, because its point of attack is not the same; error in this respect has caused many a teacher to abandon nature-study and many a pupil to hate it. In elementary science the work begins with the simplest animals and plants and progresses logically through to the highest forms; at least this is the method pursued in most universities and schools. The object of the study is to give the pupils an outlook over all the forms of life and their relation one to another. In nature-study the work begins with any plant or creature which chances to interest the pupil. It begins with the robin when it comes back to us in March, promising spring; or it begins with the maple leaf which flutters to the ground in all the beauty of its autumnal tints. A course in biological science leads to the comprehension of all kinds of life upon our globe. Nature-study is for the comprehension of the individual life of the bird, insect or plant that is nearest at hand.

Nature-study is perfectly good science within its limits, but it is not meant to be more profound or comprehensive than the capabilities of the child's mind. More than all, nature-study is not science belittled as if it were to be looked at through the reversed opera glass in or-

An Aquarium

der to bring it down small enough for the child to play with. Nature-study, as far as it goes, is just as large as is science for "grown-ups" and may deal with the same subject matter and should be characterized by the same accuracy. It simply does not go so far.

To illustrate: If we are teaching the science of ornithology, we take first the Archaeopteryx, then the swimming and the scratching birds and finally reach the song birds, studying each as a part of the whole. Nature-study begins with the robin because the child sees it and is interested in it and he notes the things about the habits and appearance of the robin that may be perceived by intimate observation. In fact, he discovers for himself all that the most advanced book of ornithology would give concerning the ordinary habits of this one bird; the next bird studied may be the turkey in the barnyard, or the duck on the pond, or the screech-owl in the spruces, if any of these happen to impinge upon his notice and interest. However, such nature-study makes for the best of scientific ornithology, because by studying the individual birds thus thoroughly, the pupil finally studies a sufficient number of forms so that his knowledge, thus assembled, gives him a better comprehension of birds as a whole than could be obtained by the routine study of the same. Nature-study does not start out with the classification given in books, but in the end it builds up a classification in the child's mind which is based on fundamental knowledge; it is a classification like that evolved by the first naturalists, it is built on careful personal observations of both form and life.

NATURE-STUDY NOT FOR DRILL

IF nature-study is made a drill, its pedagogic value is lost. When it is properly taught, the child is unconscious of mental effort or that he is suffering the act of teaching. As soon as nature-study becomes a task, it should be dropped; but how could it ever be a task to see that the sky is blue, or the dandelion golden, or to listen to the oriole in the elm!

THE CHILD NOT INTERESTED IN NATURE-STUDY

WHAT to do with the pupil not interested in nature-study subjects is a problem that confronts many earnest teachers. Usually the reason for this lack of interest, is the limited range of subjects used for nature-study lessons. Often the teacher insists upon flowers as the lesson subject, when toads or snakes would prove the key to the door of the child's interest. But whatever the cause may be, there is only one right way out of this difficulty: The child not inter-

A young entomologist

ested should be kept at his regular school work and not admitted as a member of the nature-study class, where his influence is always demoralizing. He had much better be learning his spelling lesson than learning to hate nature through being obliged to study subjects in which he is not interested. In general, it is safe to assume that the pupil's lack of interest in nature-study is owing to a fault in the teacher's method. She may be trying to fill the child's mind with facts when she should be leading him to observe these for himself, which is a most entertaining occupation for the child. It should always be borne in mind that mere curiosity is always impertinent, and that it is never more so than when exercised in the realm of nature. A genuine interest should be the basis of the study of the lives of plants and lower animals. Curiosity may elicit facts, but only real interest may mold these facts into wisdom.

WHEN TO GIVE THE LESSON

THERE are two theories concerning the time when a nature-study lesson should be given. Some teachers believe that it should be a part of the regular routine; others have found it of greatest value if reserved for that period of the school day when the pupils are weary and restless, and the teacher's nerves strained to the snapping point. The lesson on a tree, insect or flower at such a moment affords immediate relief to everyone; it is a mental excursion, from which all return refreshed and ready to finish the duties of the day.

While I am convinced that the use of the nature-study lesson for mental refreshment makes it of greatest value, yet I realize fully that if it is relegated to such periods, it may not be given at all. It might be better to give it a regular period late in the day, for there is strength and sureness in regularity. The teacher is much more likely to prepare herself for the lesson, if she knows that it is required at a certain time.

THE LENGTH OF THE LESSON

THE nature-study lesson should be short and sharp and may vary from ten minutes to a half hour in length. There should be no dawdling; if it is an observation lesson, only a few points should be noted and the meaning for the observations made clear. If an outline be suggested for field observation, it should be given in an inspiring manner which shall make each pupil anxious to see and read the truth for himself. The nature story when properly read is never finished; it is always at an interesting point, "continued in our next."

The teacher may judge as to her own progress in nature-study by the length of time she is glad to spend in reading from nature's book what is therein written. As she progresses, she finds those hours spent in studying nature speed faster, until a day thus spent seems but an hour. The author can think of nothing she would so gladly do as to spend days and months with the birds, bees and flowers with no obligation for telling what she should see. There is more than mere information in hours thus spent. Lowell describes them well when he says:

*"Those old days when the balancing of a yellow butterfly o'er a thistle bloom
Was spiritual food and lodging for the whole afternoon."*

THE NATURE-STUDY LESSON ALWAYS NEW

A nature-study lesson should not be repeated unless the pupils demand it. It should be done so well the first time that there is no need of repetition, because it has thus become a part of the child's consciousness. The repetition of the same lesson in different grades was, to begin with, a hopeless incubus upon nature-study. One disgusted boy declared, "Darn germination! I had it in the primary and last year and now I am having it again. I know *all about germination.*" The boy's attitude was a just one; but if there had been revealed to him the meaning of germination, instead of the mere process, he would have realized that until he had planted and observed every plant in the world he would not know all about germination, because each seedling has its own interesting story. The only excuse for repeating a nature-study lesson is in recalling it for comparison and contrast with other lessons. The study of the violet will naturally bring about a review of the pansy; the dandelion, of the sunflower; the horse, of the donkey; the butterfly, of the moth.

NATURE-STUDY AND OBJECT LESSONS

THE object lesson method was introduced to drill the child to see a thing accurately, not only as a whole, but in detail and to describe accurately what he saw. A book or a vase or some other object was held up before the class for a moment and then removed; afterwards the pupils described it as perfectly as possible. This is an excellent exercise and the children usually enjoy it as if it were a game. But if the teacher has in mind the same thought when she is giving the nature-study lesson, she has little comprehension of the meaning of the latter

A mountain stream

and the pupils will have less. In nature-study, it is not desirable that the child see all the details, but rather those details that have something to do with the life of the creature studied; if he sees that the grasshopper has the hind legs much longer than the others, he will inevitably note that there are two other pairs of legs and he will in the meantime have come into an illuminating comprehension of the reason the insect is called "grasshopper." The child should see definitely and accurately all that is necessary for the recognition of a plant or animal; but in nature-study, the observation of form is for the purpose of better understanding life. In fact, it is form linked with life, the relation of "being" to "doing."

NATURE-STUDY IN THE SCHOOLROOM

MANY subjects for nature-study lessons may be brought into the schoolroom. Whenever it is possible, the pupils should themselves bring the material, as the collecting of it is an important part of the lesson. There should be in the schoolroom conveniences for caring for the little prisoners brought in from the field. The terrarium and breeding cages of different kinds should be provided for the insects, toads and little mammals. Here they may live in comfort, when given their natural food, while the children observe their interesting ways. The ants' nest, and the observation hive yield fascinating views of the marvelous lives of the insect socialists, while the cheerful prisoner in the bird cage may be made a constant illustration of the adaptations and habits of all birds. The aquaria for fishes, tadpoles and insects afford the opportunity for continuous study of these water creatures and are a never-failing source of interest to the pupils, while the window garden may be made not only an ornament and an aesthetic

Observing bees

delight, but a basis for interesting study of plant growth and development.

A schoolroom thus equipped is a place of delight as well as enlightenment to the children. Once, a boy whose luxurious home was filled with all that money could buy and educated tastes select, said of a little nature-study laboratory which was in the unfinished attic of a school building, but which was teeming with life: "I think this is the most beautiful room in the world."

NATURE-STUDY AND MUSEUM SPECIMENS

THE matter of museum specimens is another question for the nature-study teacher to solve, and has a direct bearing on an attitude toward taking life. There are many who believe the stuffed bird or the case of pinned insects have no place in nature-study; and certainly these should not be the chief material. But let us use our common sense; the boy sees a bird in the woods or field and does not know its name; he seeks the bird in the museum and thus is able to place it and read about it and is stimulated to make other observations concerning it. Wherever the museum is a help to the study of life in the field, it is well and good. Some teachers may give a live lesson from a stuffed specimen, and other teachers may stuff their pupils with facts about a live specimen; of the two, the former is preferable.

There is no question that making a collection of insects is an efficient way of developing the child's powers of close observation, as well as of giving him manual dexterity in handling fragile things. Also it is a false sentiment which attributes to an insect the same agony at being impaled on a pin that we might suffer at being thrust through by a stake. The

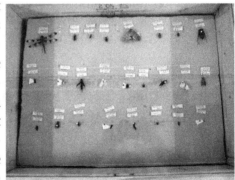

BENNY MAZUR (CC BY-SA 2.0)
Mounted insects in a box

insect nervous system is far more conveniently arranged for such an ordeal than ours; and, too, the cyanide bottle brings immediate and

13

painless death to the insects placed within it; moreover, the insects usually collected have short lives anyway. So far as the child is concerned, he is thinking of his collection of moths or butterflies and not at all of taking life; so it is not teaching him to wantonly destroy living creatures. However, an indiscriminate encouragement of the making of insect collections cannot be advised. There are some children who will profit by it and some who will not, and unquestionably the best kind of study of insects is watching their interesting ways while they live.

To kill a creature in order to prepare it for a nature-study lesson is not only wrong but absurd, for nature-study has to do with life rather than death, and the form of any creature is interesting only when its adaptations for life are studied. But again, a nature-study teacher may be an opportunist; if without any volition on her part or the pupils', a freshly killed specimen comes to hand, she should make the most of it. The writer remembers most illuminating lessons from a partridge that broke a window and its neck simultaneously during its flight one winter night, a yellow hammer that killed itself against an electric wire, and a muskrat that turned its toes to the skies for no understandable reason. In each of these cases the creature's special physical adaptations for living its own peculiar life were studied, and the effect was not the study of a dead thing, but of a successful and wonderful life.

THE LENS, MICROSCOPE, AND FIELD GLASS AS HELPS IN NATURE-STUDY

IN elementary grades, nature-study deals with objects which the children can see with the naked eye. However, a lens is a help in almost all of this work because it is such a joy to the child to gaze at the wonders it reveals. There is no lesson given in this book which requires more than a simple lens for seeing the most minute parts

Using a hand lens

Binoculars

discussed. An excellent lens may be bought for a dollar, and a fairly good one for fifty cents or even twenty-five cents. The lens should be chained to a table or desk where it may be used by the pupils at recess. This gives each an opportunity for using it and obviates the danger of losing it. If the pupils themselves own lenses, they should be fastened by a string or chain to the pocket.

A microscope has no legitimate part in nature-study. But if there is one available, it reveals so many wonders in the commonest objects, that it can be made a source of added interest ofttimes. For instance, to thus see the scales on the butterfly's wing affords the child pleasure as well as edification. Field or opera glasses, while indispensible for bird study, are by no means necessary in nature-study. However, the pupils will show greater interest in noting the birds' colors if they are allowed to make the observations with the help of a glass.

USES OF PICTURES, CHARTS, AND BLACKBOARD DRAWINGS

PICTURES alone should never be used as the subjects for nature-study lessons, but they may be of great use in illustrating and illuminating a lesson. Books well illustrated are more readily comprehended by the child and are often very helpful to him, especially after his interest in the subject is thoroughly aroused. If charts are used to illustrate the lesson, the child is likely to be misled by the size of the drawing, which is also the case in blackboard pictures. However, this error may be avoided by fixing the attention of the pupil on the object first. If the pupils are studying the ladybird and have it in their hands, the teacher may use a diagram representing the beetle as a foot long and it will still convey the idea accurately; but if she begins with the picture, she probably can never convince the children that the picture has anything to do with the insect.

In making blackboard drawings illustrative of the lesson, it is best, if possible, to have one of the pupils do the drawing in the presence of the class; or, if the teacher does the drawing, she should hold the object in her hand while doing it and look at it often so that the children may see that she is trying to represent it accurately. Taking everything into consideration, however, nature-study charts and blackboard drawings are of little use to the nature-study teacher.

THE USES OF SCIENTIFIC NAMES

DISQUIETING problems relative to scientific nomenclature always confront the teacher of nature-study. My own practice has been to use the popular names of species, except in cases where confusion might ensue, and to use the scientific names for anatomical parts. However, this matter is of little importance if the teacher bears in mind that the purpose of nature-study is to know the subject under observation and to learn the name incidentally.

If the teacher says: "I have a pink hepatica. Can anyone find me a blue one?" the children, who naturally like grown-up words, will soon be calling these flowers hepaticas. But if the teacher says, "These flowers are called hepaticas. Now please everyone remember the name. Write it in your books as I write it on the blackboard,

Common tree frog or tree toad, Hyla versicolor. *Another species,* Hyla crucifer, *is also often called the tree frog and tree toad. Common names, then, will not distinguish these amphibians one from another; the scientific names must be applied.*

and in half an hour I shall ask you again what it is," the pupils naturally look upon the exercise as a word lesson and its real significance is lost. This sort of nature-study is dust and ashes and there has been too much of it. The child should never be *required* to learn the name of anything in the nature-study work; but the name should be used so often and so naturally in his presence, that he will learn it without being conscious of the process.

THE STORY AS A SUPPLEMENT TO THE
NATURE-STUDY LESSON

MANY of the subjects for nature lessons can be studied only in part, since but one phase may be available at the time. Often, especially if there is little probability that the pupils will find opportunity to complete the study, it is best to round out their knowledge by reading or telling the story to supplement the facts which they have discovered for themselves. This story should not be told as a finality or as a complete picture but as a guide and inspiration for further study. Always leave at the end of the story an interrogation mark that will remain aggressive and insistent in the child's mind. To illustrate: Once a club of junior naturalists brought me rose leaves injured by the leaf-cutter bee and asked me why the leaves were cut out so regularly. I told them the story of the use made by the mother bee of these oval and circular bits of leaves and made the account as vital as I was able; but at the end I said, "I do not know which species of bee cut these leaves. She is living here among us and building her nest with your rose leaves which she is cutting every day almost under your very eyes. Is she then so much more clever than you that you cannot see her nor find her nest?" For two years following this lesson I received letters from members of this club. Two carpenter bees and their nests were discovered by them and studied before the mysterious leaf-cutter was finally ferreted out. My story had left something interesting for the young naturalists to discover. The children should be impressed with the fact that the nature story is never finished. There is not a weed nor an insect nor a tree so common that the child, by observing carefully, may not see things never yet recorded in scientific books; therefore the supplementary story should be made an inspiration for keener interest and

GAIL HAMPSHIRE (CC BY-SA 2.0)
The leaf-cutter bee

ration for keener interest and further investigation on the part of the pupil. The supplementary story simply thrusts aside some of the obscuring underbrush thus revealing more plainly the path to further knowledge.

THE NATURE-STUDY ATTITUDE TOWARD LIFE AND DEATH

PERHAPS no greater danger besets the pathway of the nature-study teacher than the question involved in her pupils' attitude toward life and death. To inculcate in the child a reverence for life and yet to keep him from becoming mawkish and morbid is truly a problem. It is almost inevitable that the child should become sympathetic with the life of the animal or plant studied, since a true understanding of the life of any creature creates an interest which stimulates a desire to protect this particular creature and make its life less hard. Many times, within my own experience, have I known boys, who began by robbing birds' nests for egg collections, to end by becoming most zealous protectors of the birds. The humane qualities within these boys budded and blossomed in the growing knowledge of the lives of the birds. At Cornell University, it is a well known fact that those students who turn aside so as not to crush the ant, caterpillar or cricket on the pavement are almost invariably those that are studying entomology; and in America it is the botanists themselves who are leading the crusade for flower protection.

Thus, the nature-study teacher, if she does her work well, is a sure aid in inculcating a respect for the rights of all living beings to their own lives; and she needs only to lend her influence gently in this direction to change carelessness to thoughtfulness and cruelty to kindness. But with this impetus toward a reverence for life, the teacher soon finds herself in a dilemma from which there is no logical way out, so long as she lives in a world where lamb chop, beefsteak and roast chicken are articles of ordinary diet; a world in fact, where every meal is based upon the death of some creature. For if she places much emphasis upon the sacredness of life, the children soon begin to question whether it be right to slay the lamb or the chicken for their own food. It would seem that there is nothing for the consistent nature-study teacher to do but become a vegetarian, and even then there might arise refinements in this question of taking life; she might have to consider the cruelty to asparagus in cutting it off in plump infancy, or the ethics of devouring in the turnip the food laid up by the mother plant to perfect her seed. In fact, a most rigorous diet would be forced upon the teacher who should refuse to sustain her own existence at the cost of life; and if she should attempt to teach the righteousness of such a diet she would undoubtedly forfeit her position; and yet what is she to do! She will soon find herself in the position of a certain lady who placed sheets of sticky fly-paper around her kitchen to rid her house of flies, and then in mental anguish picked off the buzzing, struggling victims and sought to clean their too adhesive wings and legs.

In fact, drawing the line between what to kill and what to let live, requires the use of common sense rather than logic. First of all, the nature-study teacher, while exemplifying and encouraging the humane attitude toward the lower creatures, and repressing cruelty which wantonly causes suffering, should never magnify the terrors of death. Death is as natural as life and the inevitable end of physical life on our globe. Therefore, every story and every sentiment expressed which makes the child feel that death is terrible, is wholly wrong. The one right way to teach about death is not to emphasize it one way or another, but to deal with it as a circumstance common to all; it should be no more emphasized than the fact that creatures eat or fall asleep.

Another thing for the nature-study teacher to do is to direct the interest of the child so that it shall center upon the hungry creature rather than upon the one which is made into the meal. It is well to emphasize the fact that one of the conditions imposed upon every living being in the woods and fields, is that it is entitled to a meal when it is hungry, if it is clever enough to get it. The child naturally takes this view of it. I remember well as a child I never thought particularly about the mouse which my cat was eating; in fact, the process of transmuting mouse into cat seemed altogether proper, but when the cat played with the mouse, that was quite another thing, and was never permitted. Although no one appreciates more deeply than I the debt which we owe to Thompson-Seton and writers of his kind, who have placed before the public the animal story from the animal point of view and thus set us all to thinking, yet it is certainly wrong to impress this view too strongly upon the young and sensitive child. In fact, this process should not begin until the judgment and the understanding is well developed, for we all know that although seeing the other fellow's standpoint is a source of strength and breadth of mind, yet living the other fellow's life is, at best, an enfeebling process and a futile waste of energy.

SHOULD THE NATURE-STUDY TEACHER TEACH
HOW TO DESTROY LIFE?

IT IS probably within the proper scope of the nature-study teacher to place emphasis upon the domain of man, who being the most powerful of all animals, asserts his will as to which ones shall live in his midst. From a standpoint of abstract justice, the stray cat has just as much right to kill and eat the robin which builds in the vine of my porch as the robin has to pull and eat the earthworms from my lawn; but the place is mine, and I choose to kill the cat and preserve the robin.

When emphasizing the domain of man, we may have to deal with the killing of creatures which are injurious to his interests. Nature-study may be tributary to this, in a measure, and indirectly, but it is surely *not* nature-study. For example, the child studies the cabbage butterfly in all its stages, the exquisitely sculptured yellow egg, the velvety green caterpillar, the chrysalis with its protecting colors, the white-winged butterfly, and becomes interested in the life of the insect. Not under any consideration, when the attention of the child is focused on the insect, should we suggest a remedy for it when a pest. Let the life-story of the butterfly stand as a fascinating page of nature's book. But later, when the child enters on his career as a gardener, when he sets out his row of cabbage plants and waters and cultivates them, and does his best to bring them to maturity, along comes the butterfly, now an arch enemy, and begins to rear her progeny on the product of his toil. Now the child's interest is focused on the cabbage, and the question is not one of killing insects so much as of saving plants. In fact, there is nothing in spraying the plants with Paris green which suggests cruelty to innocent caterpillars, nor is the process likely to harden the child's sensibilities.

To gain knowledge of the life-story of insects or other creatures is nature-study. To destroy them as pests is a part of Agriculture or Horticulture. The one may be of fundamental assistance to the other, but the two are quite separate and should never be confused.

THE FIELD NOTEBOOK

A field note-book may be made a joy to the pupil and a help to the teacher. Any kind of a blank book will do for this, except that it should not be too large to be carried in the pocket, and it should always have the pencil attached. To make the note-book a success the following rules should be observed:

(a) The book should be considered the personal property of the child and should never be criticized by the teacher except as a matter of encouragement; for the spirit in which the notes are made, is more important than the information they cover.

(b) The making of drawings should be encouraged for illustrating what is observed. A graphic drawing is far better than a long description of a natural object.

(c) The note-book should not be regarded as a part of the work in English. The spelling, language and writing of the notes should all be exempt from criticism.

(d) As occasion offers, outlines for observing certain plants or animals may be placed in the note-book previous to the field excursion so as to give definite points for the work.

(e) No child should be compelled to have a note-book.

The field note-book is a veritable gold mine for the nature-study teacher to work, in securing voluntary and happy observations from the pupils concerning their out-of-door interests. It is a friendly gate which admits the teacher to a knowledge of what the child sees and cares for. Through it she may discover where the child's attention impinges upon the realm of nature and thus may know where to find the starting point for cultivating larger intelligence and a wider interest.

I have examined many field note-books kept by pupils in the intermediate grades and have been surprised at their plenitude of accurate observation and graphic illustration. These books ranged from blank account books furnished by the family grocer up to a quarto, the pages of which were adorned with many marginal illustrations made in passionate admiration of Thompson-Seton's books and filled with carefully transcribed text, that showed the direct influence of Thoreau. These books, of whatever quality, are precious beyond price to their owners. And why not? For they represent what cannot be bought or sold, personal experience in the happy world of out-of-doors.

Chapter XXV

January

A page in the field note-book of a lad of fourteen who read Thoreau and admired the books of Thompson-Seton.

THE FIELD EXCURSION

MANY teachers look upon the field excursion as a precarious voyage, steered between the Scylla of hilarious seeing too much and the Charybdis of seeing nothing at all because of the zest which comes from freedom in the fields and wood. This danger can be obviated if the teacher plans the work definitely before starting, and demands certain results.

It is a mistake to think that a half day is necessary for a field lesson, since a very efficient field trip may be made during the ten or fifteen minutes at recess, if it is well planned. Certain questions and lines of investigation should be given the pupils before starting and given in such a manner as to make them

A brook in winter

thoroughly interested in discovering the facts. A certain teacher in New York State has studied all the common plants and trees in the vicinity of her school with these recess excursions and the pupils have been enthusiastic about the work.

The half hour excursion should be preceded by a talk concerning the purposes of the outing and the pupils must know that certain observations are to be made or they will not be permitted to go again. This should not be emphasized as a punishment; but they should be made to understand that a field excursion is only, naturally enough, for those who wish to see and understand outdoor life. For all field work, the teacher should make use of the field notebook which should be a part of the pupils' equipment.

PETS AS NATURE-STUDY SUBJECTS

LITTLE attention has been given to making the child understand what would be the lives of his pets if they were in their native environment; or to relating their habits and lives as wild animals. Almost any pet, if properly observed, affords an admirable opportunity for understanding the reasons why its structure and peculiar habits may have made it successful among other creatures and in other lands.

Moreover the actions and the daily life of the pet make interesting subject matter for a note-book. The lessons on the dog, rabbit and horse as given in this volume may suggest methods for such study, and with apologies that it is not better and more interesting, I have

Young guinea pig

placed with the story of the squirrel a few pages from one of my own note-books regarding my experiences with "Furry." I include this record as a suggestion for the children that they should keep note-books of their pets. It will lead them to closer observation and to a better and more natural expression of their experiences.

THE CORRELATION OF NATURE-STUDY WITH LANGUAGE WORK

NATURE-STUDY should be so much a part of the child's thought and interest that it will naturally form a thought core for other subjects quite unconsciously on his part. In fact, there is one safe rule for correlation in this case, it is legitimate and excellent training as long as the pupil does not discover that he is correlating. But there is something in human nature which revolts against doing one thing to accomplish quite another. A boy once said to me, "I'd rather never go on a field excursion than to have to write it up for English," a sentiment I sympathized with keenly; ulterior motive is sickening to the honest spirit. But if that same boy had been a member of a field class and had enjoyed all the new experiences and had witnessed the interesting things discovered on this excursion, and if later his teacher had asked him to write for her an account of some part of it, because *she wished to know what he had discovered*, the chances are that he would have written his story joyfully and with a certain pride that would have counted much for achievement in word expression.

When Mr. John Spencer, known to so many children in New York State as "Uncle John," was conducting the Junior Naturalist Clubs, the teachers allowed letters to him to count for language exercises; and the eagerness with which these letters were written should have given the teachers the key to the proper method of teaching English. Mr. Spencer requested the teachers not to correct the letters, because he wished the children to be thinking about the subject matter rather than the form of expression. But so anxious were many of the pupils to make their letters perfect, that they earnestly requested their teachers to help them write correctly, which was an ideal condition for teaching them English. Writing letters to Uncle John was such a joy to the pupils that it was used as a privilege and a reward of merit in many schools. One rural teacher reduced the percentage of tardiness to a minimum by giving the first period in the morning to the work in English which consisted of letters to Uncle John.

Why do pupils dislike writing English exercises? Simply because they are not interested in the subject they are asked to write about, and they know that the teacher is not interested in the information contained in the essay. But when they are interested in the subject and write about it to a person who is interested, the conditions are entirely changed. If the teacher, overwhelmed as she is by work and perplexities, could only keep in mind that the purpose of a language is, after all, merely to convey ideas, some of her perplexities would fade away. A conveyance naturally should be fitted for the load it is to carry, and if the pupil acquires the load first he is very likely to construct a conveyance that will be adequate. How often the conveyance is made perfect through much effort and polished through agony of spirit and the load entirely forgotten!

Nature-study lessons give much excellent subject matter for stories and essays, but these essays should never be criticized or defaced with the blue pencil. They should be read with interest by the teacher; the mistakes made in them, so transformed as to be unrecognizable, may be used for drill exercises in grammatical construction. After all, grammar and spelling are only gained by practice and there is no royal road leading to their acquirement.

THE CORRELATION OF NATURE-STUDY AND DRAWING

THE correlation of nature-study and drawing is so natural and inevitable that it needs never be revealed to the pupil. When the child is interested in studying any object, he enjoys illustrating his observations with drawings; the happy absorption of children thus engaged is a delight to witness. At its best, drawing is a perfectly natural method of self-expression. The savage and the young child, both untutored, seek to express themselves and their experiences by this means. It is only when the object to be drawn is foreign to the interest of the child that drawing is a task.

Nature-study offers the best means for bridging the gap that lies between the kindergarten child who makes drawings because he loves to and is impelled to from within, and the pupil in the grades who is obliged to draw what the teacher places before him. From making crude and often meaningless pencil strokes, which is the entertainment of the young child, the outlining of a leaf or some other simple and interesting natural object, is a normal step full of interest for the child because it is still self-expression.

A mounted fern

Miss Mary E. Hill gives every year in the Goodyear School of Syracuse an exhibition of the drawings made by the children in the nature-study classes; and these are universally so excellent that most people regard them as an exhibition from the Art Department; and yet many of these pupils have never had lessons in drawing. They have learned to draw because they like to make pictures of the living objects which they have studied. One year there were many pictures of toads in various stages in this exhibit, and although their anatomy was sometimes awry in the pictures, yet there was a certain vivid expression of life in their representation; one felt that the toads could jump. Miss Hill allows the pupils to choose their own medium, pencil, crayon, or water-color, and says that they seem to feel which is best. For instance, when drawing the outline of trees in winter they choose pencil, but when representing the trillium or iris they prefer the water-color, while for bitter-sweet and crocuses they choose the colored crayons.

It is through this method of drawing that which interests him, that the child retains and keeps as his own, what should be an inalienable right, a graphic method of expressing his own impressions. Too much have we emphasized drawing as an art; it may be an art, if the one who draws is an artist; but if he is not an artist he still has a right to draw if it pleases him to do so. We might as well declare that a child should not speak unless he put his words into poetry, as to declare that he should not draw because his drawings are not artistic.

THE CORRELATION OF NATURE-STUDY WITH GEOGRAPHY

LIFE depends upon its environment. Geographical conditions and limitations have shaped the mold into which plastic life has been poured and by which its form has been modified. It may be easy for the untrained mind to see how the deserts and oceans affect life. Cattle may not roam in the former because there is nothing there for them to eat, nor may they occupy the latter because they are not fitted for breathing air in the water. And yet the camel can endure thirst and live on the scant food of the desert; and the whale is a mammal fitted to live in the sea. The question is, how are we to impress the child with the "have to" which lies behind all these geographical facts. If animals live in the desert they *have to* subsist on scant and peculiar food which grows there; they *have to* get along with little water; they *have to* endure heat and sand storms; they *have to* have eyes that will not become blinded by the vivid reflection of the sunlight on the sand; they *have to* be of sand color so that they may escape the eyes of their enemies or creep upon their prey unperceived.

All these have to's are not mere chance, but they have existed so long that the animal, by constantly coming in contact with them, has attained its present form and habits.

There are just as many have to's in the stream or the pond back of the school-house, on the dry hillside behind it or in the woods beyond the creek as

MARTURIUS (CC BY-SA 3.0)
A meandering stream

there are in desert or ocean; and when the child gets an inkling of this fact, he has made a great step into the realm of geography. When he realizes why water lilies can grow only in still water that is not too deep and which has a silt bottom, and why the cat-tails grow in swamps where there is not too much water, and why the mullein grows in the dry pasture, and why the hepatica thrives in the rich, damp woods, and why the daisies grow in the meadows, he will understand that this partnership of nature and geography illustrates the laws which govern life. Many phases of physical geography belong to the realm of nature-study; the brook, its course, its work or erosion and sedimentation; the rocks of many kinds, the soil, the climate, the weather, are all legitimate subjects for nature-study lessons.

THE CORRELATION OF NATURE-STUDY WITH HISTORY

THERE are many points where nature-study impinges upon history in a way that may prove the basis for an inspiring lesson. Many of our weeds, cultivated plants and domestic animals have been introduced from Europe and are a part of our colonial history; while there are many of the most commonly seen creatures which have played their part in the history of ancient times. For instance, the bees which gave to man the only means available to him for sweetening his food until the 17th century, were closely allied to the home life of ancient peoples. The buffalo which ranged our western plains had much to do with the life of the red man. The study of the grasshopper brings to the child's attention stories of the locusts' invasion mentioned in the Bible, and the stars, which witnessed our creation and of which Job sang and the ancients wrote, shine over our heads every night.

But the trees, through the lengthy span of their lives, cover more history individually, than do other organisms. In glancing across the wood-covered hills of New York one often sees there, far above the other trees, the gaunt crowns of old white pines. Such trees belonged to the forest primeval and may have attained the age of two centuries; they stand there looking out over the world, relics of another age when America belonged to the red man, and the bear and the panther played or fought beneath them. The cedars live longer than do the pines and the great scarlet oak may have attained the age of four centuries before it yields to fate.

Perhaps in no other way may the attention of the pupil be turned so naturally to past events, as through the thought that the life of such a tree has spanned so much of human history. The life history of one of these ancient trees should be made the center of local history; let the pupils find

The treaty oak in Austin, Texas. This was once part of fourteen oak tress that served as a sacred meeting place for Comanche and Tonkawa tribes prior to European settlement.

when the town was first settled by the whites and where they came from and how large the tree was then. What Indian tribes roamed the woods before that and what animals were common in the forest when this tree was a sapling? Thus may be brought out the chief events in the history of the county and township, when they were established and for whom or what they were named; and a comparison of the present industries may be made with those of a hundred years ago.

THE CORRELATION OF NATURE-STUDY WITH ARITHMETIC

THE arithmetical problems presented by nature-study are many; some of them are simple and some of them are complicated, and all of them are illumining. Seed distribution especially lends itself to computation; a milkweed pod contains 140 seeds; there are five such pods on one plant, each milkweed plant requires at least one square foot of ground to grow on; how much ground would be required to grow all of the seeds from this one plant? Or, count the seeds in one dandelion head, multiply by the number of flower heads on the plant and estimate how many plants can grow on a square foot, then ask a boy how long it would take for one dandelion plant to cover his father's farm with its progeny; or count the blossoms on one branch of an apple tree, later count the ripened fruit; what percentage of blossoms ma-

A spreading banyan tree

tured into fruit? Measuring trees, their height and thickness and computing the lumber they will make combines arithmetic and geometry, and so on *ad infinitum.*

As a matter of fact, the teacher will find in almost every nature lesson an arithmetic lesson; and when arithmetic is used in this work, it should be vital and inherent and not "tacked on;" the pupils should be really interested in the answers to their problems; and as with all correlation, the success of it depends upon the genius of the teacher.

GARDENING AND NATURE-STUDY

ERRONEOUSLY, some people maintain that gardening is nature-study; this is not so necessarily nor ordinarily. Gardening may be a basis for nature-study but it is rarely made so to any great extent. Even the work in children's gardens is so conducted that the pupils know little or nothing of the flowers or vegetables which they grow except their names, their uses to man and how to cultivate them. They are taught how to prepare the soil, but the reason for this from the plant's standpoint is never revealed; and if the child becomes acquainted with the plants in his garden, he makes the discovery by himself. All this is nothing against gardening! It is a wholesome and valuable experience for a child to learn how to make a garden even if he remains ignorant of the interesting facts concerning the plants which he there cultivates. But if the teachers are so inclined, they may find in the garden and its products, the most interesting material for the best of nature lessons. Every plant the child grows is an individual with its own peculiarities as well as those of its species in manner of growth. Its roots, stems and leaves are of certain form and structure; and often the special uses to the plant of its own kind of leaves, stems and roots are obvious. Each plant has its own form of flower and even its own tricks for securing pollenation; and its own manner of developing and scattering its seeds. Every weed of the garden has developed some special method of winning and holding its place among the cultivated plants; and in no other way may the child so fully and naturally come into a comprehension of that term "the survival of the fittest" as by studying the ways of the fit as exemplified in the triumphant weeds of his garden.

Every earthworm working below the soil is doing something for the garden. Every bee that visits the flowers there is on an errand for the garden as well as for herself. Every insect feeding on leaf or root is doing something to the garden. Every bird that nests near by or that ever visits it, is doing something which affects the life and the growth of the garden. What all of these uninvited guests are doing is one field of garden nature-study. Aside from all this study of individual life in the garden which even the youngest child may take part in, there are the more advanced lessons on the soil. What kind of soil is it? From what sort of rock was it formed? What renders it mellow and fit for the growing of plants? Moreover, what do the plants get from it? How do they get it? What do they do with what they get?

This leads to the subject of plant physiology, the elements of which may be taught simply by experiments carried on by the children themselves, experiments which should demonstrate the sap currents in the plant; the use of water to carry food and in making the plant rigid; the use of sunshine in making the plant food in the leaf laboratories; the nourishment provided for the seed and its germination, and many other similar lessons.

A child who makes a garden, and thus becomes intimate with the plants he cultivates, and comes to understand the interrelation of the various forms of life which he finds in his garden, has progressed far in the fundamental knowledge of nature's ways as well as in a practical knowledge of agriculture.

NATURE-STUDY AND AGRICULTURE

LUCKILY, thumb-rule agriculture is being pushed to the wall in these enlightened days. Thumb rules would work much better if nature did not vary her performances in such a confusing way. Government experiment stations were established because thumb rules for farming were unreliable and disappointing; and all the work of all the experiment stations has been simply advanced nature-study and its application to the practice of agriculture. Both nature-study and agriculture are based upon the study of life and the physical conditions which encourage or limit life; this is known to the world as the study of the natural sciences; and if we see clearly the relation of nature-study to science, we may understand better the relation of nature-study to agriculture, which is based upon the sciences.

Nature-study is science brought home. It is a knowledge of botany, zoology and geology as illustrated in the dooryard, the corn-field or the woods back of the house. Some people have an idea that to know these sciences one must go to college; they do not understand that nature has furnished the material and laboratories on every farm in the land. Thus, by beginning with the child in nature-study we take him to the laboratory of the wood or garden, the roadside or the field, and his materials are the wild flowers or the weeds, or the insects that visit the golden-rod or the bird that sings in the maple tree, or the woodchuck whistling in the pasture. The child begins to study living things anywhere or everywhere, and his progress is always along the various tracks laid down by the laws of life, along which his work as an agriculturist must always progress if it is to be successful.

The child through nature-study learns the way a plant grows, whether it be an oak, a turnip or a pigweed; he learns how the roots of each is adapted to its needs; how the leaves place themselves to get the sunshine and why they need it; and how the flowers get their pollen carried by the bee or wind; and how the seeds are finally scattered and planted. Or he learns about the life of the bird, whether it be a chicken, an owl or a bobolink; he knows how each bird gets its food and what its food is, where it lives, where it nests and its relation to other living things. He studies the bumblebee and discovers its great mission of pollen carrying for many flowers, and in the end would

Bales of straw

no sooner strike it dead than he would voluntarily destroy his clover patch. This is the kind of learning we call nature-study and not science or agriculture. But the country child can never learn anything in nature-study that has not something to do with science; and that has not its own practical lesson for him, when he shall become a farmer.

Some have argued, "Why not make nature-study along the lines of agriculture solely? Why should not the child begin nature-study with the cabbage rather than the wild flowers?" This argument carried out logically provides recreation for a boy in hoeing corn rather than in playing ball. Many parents in the past have argued thus and have, in consequence, driven thousands of splendid boys from the country to the city with a loathing in their souls for the drudgery which seemed all there was to farm life. The reason why the wild flowers may be selected for beginning the nature-study of plants, is because every child loves these woodland posies, and his happiest hours are spent in gathering them. Never yet have we known of a case where a child having gained his knowledge of the way a plant lives through studying the plants he loves, has failed to be interested and delighted to find that the wonderful things he discovered about his wild flower may be true of the vegetable in the garden, or the purslane which fights with it for ground to stand upon.

Some have said, "We, as farmers, care only to know what concerns our pocket-books; we wish only to study those things which we must, as farmers, cultivate or destroy. We do not care for the butterfly, but we wish to know the plum weevil; we do not care for the trillium but

Straw bales at harvest time

we are interested in the onion; we do not care for the meadow-lark but we cherish the gosling." This is an absurd argument since it is a mental impossibility for any human being to discriminate between two things when he knows or sees only one. In order to understand the important economic relations to the world of one plant or animal, it is absolutely necessary to have a wide knowledge of other plants and animals. One might as well say, "I will see the approaching cyclone, but never look at the sky; I will look at the clover but not see the dandelion; I will look for the sheriff when he comes over the hill but will not see any other team on the road."

Nature-study is an effort to make the individual use his senses instead of losing them; to train him to keep his eyes open to all things so that his powers of discrimination shall be based on wisdom. The ideal farmer is not the man who by hazard and chance succeeds; he is the man who loves his farm and all that surrounds it because he is awake to the beauty as well as to the wonders which are there; he is the man who understands as far as may be the great forces of nature which are at work around him, and therefore, he is able to make them work for him. For what is agriculture save a diversion of natural forces for the benefit of man! The farmer who knows these forces only when restricted to his paltry crops, and has no idea of their larger application, is no more efficient as a father than would a man be as an engineer who knew nothing of his engine except how to start and stop it.

In order to appreciate truly his farm, the farmer must needs begin as a child with nature-study; in order to be successful and make the farm pay, he must needs continue in nature-study; and to make his declining years happy, content, full of wide sympathies and profitable thought, he must needs conclude with nature-study; for nature-study is the alphabet of agriculture and no word in that great vocation may be spelled without it.

NATURE-STUDY CLUBS

THE organizing of a club by the pupils for the purpose of studying out-of-door life, is a great help and inspiration to the work in nature-study in the classroom. The essays and the talks before the club, prove efficient aid in English composition; and the varied interests of the members of the club, furnish new and vital material for study. A button or a badge may be designed for the club and, of course, it must have constitution and by-laws. The proceedings of the club meetings should be conducted according to parliamentary rules; but the field excursions should be entirely informal.

The meetings of the Junior Naturalists Clubs, as organized in the schools of New York State by Mr. John W. Spencer, were most impressive. The school session would be brought to a close, the teacher stepping down and taking a seat with the pupils. The president of the club, some bashful boy or slender slip of a girl, would take the chair and conduct the meeting with a dignity and efficiency worthy of a statesman. The order was perfect, the discussion much to the point. I confess to a feeling of awe when I attended these meetings, conducted so seriously and so formally, by such youngsters. Undoubtedly, the parliamentary training and experience in speaking impromptu, are among the chief benefits of such a club.

These clubs may be organized for special study. In one bird club of which I know there have been contests. Sides were chosen and the number of birds seen from May 1st to 31st inclusive was the test of supremacy. Notes on the birds were taken in the field with such care, that when at the end of the month each member handed in his notes, they could be used as evidence of accurate identification. An umpire with the help of bird manuals decided the doubtful points. This year the score stood 79 to 81.

The programs of the nature club should be varied so as to be continually interesting. Poems and stories, concerning the objects studied, help make the program attractive.

HOW TO USE THIS BOOK

FIRST and indispensably, the teacher should have at hand the subject of the lesson. She should make herself familiar with the points covered by the questions and read the story before giving the lesson. If she does not have the time to go over the observations suggested, before giving the lesson, she should take up the questions with the pupils as a joint investigation, and be boon companion in discovering the story.

The story should not be read to the pupils. It is given as an assistance to the teacher, and is not meant for direct information to the pupils. If the teacher knows a fact in nature's realm, she is then in a position to lead her pupils to discover this fact for themselves.

Make the lesson an investigation and make the pupils feel that they are investigators. To tell the story to begin with, inevitably spoils this attitude and quenches interest.

The "leading thought" embodies some of the points which should be in the teacher's mind while giving the lesson; it should not be read or declared to the pupils.

The outlines for observations herein given, by no means cover all of the observations possible; they are meant to suggest to the teacher observations of her own, rather than to be followed slavishly.

The suggestions for observations have been given in the form of questions, merely for the sake of saving space. The direct questioning method, if not employed with discretion, becomes tiresome to both pupil and teacher. If the questions do not inspire the child to investigate, they are useless. To grind out answers to questions about any natural object is not nature-study, it is simply "grind," a form of mental activity which is of much greater use when applied to spelling or the multiplication table than to the study of nature. The best teacher will cover the points suggested for observations with few direct questions. To those who find the questions inadequate I will say that, although I have used these outlines once, I am sure I should never be able to use them again without making changes.

The topics chosen for these lessons may not be the most practical nor the most interesting nor the most enlightening that are to be found; they are simply those subjects which I have used in my classes, because we happened to find them at hand the mornings the lessons were given.

While an earnest attempt has been made to make the information in this book accurate, it is to be expected and to be hoped that many discrepancies will be found by those who follow the lessons. No two animals or plants are just alike, and no two people see things exactly the same way. *The chief aim of this volume is to encourage investigation rather than to give information.* Therefore, if mistakes are found, the object of the book will have been accomplished, and the author will feel deeply gratified. If the teacher finds that the observations made by her and her pupils, do not agree with the statements in the book, I earnestly enjoin upon her to trust to her own eyes rather than to any book.

No teacher is expected to teach all the lessons in this book. A wide range of subjects is given, so that congenial choice may be made.

An old mulberry tree

A loggerhead shrike adult feeding some recent fledglings

BIRDS

THE reason for studying any bird is to ascertain what it does; in order to accomplish this, it is necessary to know what the bird is, learning what it is, being simply a step that leads to a knowledge of what it does. But, to hear some of our bird devotees talk, one would think that to be able to identify a bird is all of bird study. On the contrary, the identification of birds is simply the alphabet to the real study, the alphabet by means of which we may spell out the life habits of the bird. To know these habits is the ambition of the true ornithologist, and should likewise be the ambition of the beginner, even though the beginner be a young child.

Several of the most common birds have been selected as subjects for lessons in this book; other common birds, like the phoebe and wrens, have been omitted purposely; after the children have studied the birds, as indicated in the lessons, they will enjoy working out lessons for themselves with other birds. Naturally, the sequence of these lessons does not follow scientific classification; in the first ten lessons, an attempt has been made to lead the child gradually into a knowledge of bird life. Beginning with the chicken there follow naturally the lessons with pigeons and the canary; then there follows the careful

These 20 day old barn swallows are starting to take small test flights but are still being fed in the nest.

and detailed study of the robins and constant comparison of them with the blue birds. This is enough for the first year in the primary grades. The next year the work begins with the birds that remain in the North during the winter, the chickadee, nuthatch and downy woodpecker. After these have been studied carefully, the teacher may be an opportunist when spring comes and select any of the lessons when the bird subjects are at hand. The classification suggested for the woodpeckers and the swallows is for more advanced pupils, as are the lessons on the geese and turkeys. It is to be hoped that these lessons will lead the child directly to the use of the bird manuals, of which there are several excellent ones.

Beginning Bird Study in the Primary Grades

The hen is especially adapted as an object lesson for the young beginner of bird study. First of all, she is a bird, notwithstanding the adverse opinions of two of my small pupils who stoutly maintained that "a robin is a bird, but a hen is a hen." Moreover, the hen is a bird always available for nature-study; she looks askance at us from the crates of the world's marts; she comes to meet us in the country barnyard, stepping toward us sedately; looking at us earnestly, with one eye, then turning her head so as to check up her observations with the other; meantime she asks us a little question in a wheedling, soft tone, which we understand perfectly to mean "have you perchance brought me something to eat?" Not only is the hen an interesting bird in her-

A commong blackbird (Turdus merula) *on her nest.*

self, but she is a bird with problems; and by studying her carefully we may be introduced into the very heart and center of bird life.

This lesson may be presented in two ways: First, if the pupils live in the country where they have poultry at home, the whole series of lessons may best be accomplished through interested talks on the part of the teacher, which should be followed on the part of the children, by observations, which should be made at home and the results given in school in oral or written lessons. Second, if the pupils are not familiar with fowls, a hen and a chick, if possible, should be kept in a cage in the schoolroom for a few days, and a duck or gosling should be brought in one day for observation. The crates in which fowls are sent to market make very good cages. One of the teachers of the Elmira, N. Y. Schools introduced into the basement of the schoolhouse a hen, which there hatched her brood of chicks, much to the children's delight and edification. After the pupils have become thoroughly interested in the hen and are familiar with her ways, after they have fed her and watched her, and have for her a sense of ownership, the following lessons may be given in an informal manner, as if they were naturally suggested to the teacher's mind through watching the fowl.

Feathers as Clothing

THE bird's clothing affords a natural beginning for bird study because the wearing of feathers is a most striking character distinguishing birds from other creatures; also, feathers and flying are the first things the young child notices about birds.

The purpose of all of these lessons on the hen are: (a) To induce the child to make continued and sympathetic observations on the habits of the domestic birds. (b) To cause him involuntarily to compare the domestic with the wild birds. (c) To induce him to think for himself why the shape of the body, wings, head, beak, feet, legs and feathers are adapted in each species to protect the bird and assist it in getting its living.

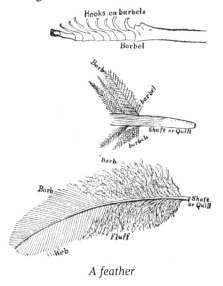

A feather

The overlapping of the feathers on a hen's back and breast is a pretty illustration of nature's method of shingling, so that the rain, finding no place to enter, drips off, leaving the bird's underclothing quite dry. It is interesting to note how a hen behaves in the rain; she droops her tail and holds herself so that the water finds upon her no resting place, but simply a steep surface down which to flow to the ground.

Each feather consists of three parts, the shaft or quill, which is the central stiff stem of the feather, giving it strength. From this quill come off the barbs which, toward the outer end, join together in a smooth web, making the thin, fan-like portion of the feather; at the base is the fluff, which is soft and downy and near to the body of the fowl. The teacher should put on the blackboard this figure so that incidentally the pupils may learn the parts of a feather and their struc-

Feathers help birds to endure the cold.

ture. If a microscope is available, show both the web and the fluff of a feather under a three-fourths objective.

The feathers on the back of a hen are longer and narrower in proportion than those on the breast and are especially fitted to protect the back from rain; the breast feathers are shorter and have more of the fluff, thus protecting the breast from the cold as well as the rain. It is plain to any child that the soft fluff is comparable to our woolen underclothing while the smooth, overlapping web forms a rain and wind-proof outer coat. Down is a feather with no quill; young chicks are covered with down. A pin-feather is simply a young feather rolled up in a sheath, which bursts later and is shed, leaving the feather free to assume its form. Take a large pin-feather and cut the sheath open and show the pupils the young feather lying within.

When a hen oils her feathers it is a process well worth observing. The oil gland is on her back just at the base of the tail feathers; she squeezes the gland with her beak to get the oil and then rubs the beak over the surface of her feathers and passes them through it; she spends more time oiling the feathers on her back and breast than those on the other parts, so that they will surely shed water. Country people say when the hen oils her feathers, it is a sure sign of rain. The hen sheds her feathers once a year and is a most untidy looking bird meanwhile, a fact that she seems to realize, and is as shy and cross as a young lady caught in company in curl papers; but she seems very pleased with herself when she finally gains her new feathers.

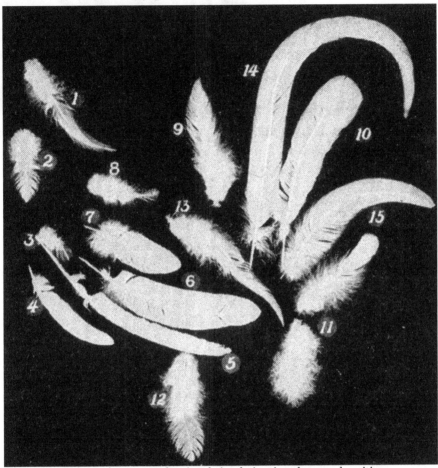

Feathers of a rooster, showing their relative size, shape and position.

1. neck hackle; 2. breast; 3. wing shoulder covert; 4. wing flight covert; 5. wing primary; 6. wing secondary; 7. wing covert; 8. back; 9. tail covert; 10. main tail; 11. fluff; 12. thigh; 13. saddle hackle; 14. the sickle or feather of beauty; 15. lesser sickle.

Leading thought— Feathers grow from the skin of a bird and protect the bird from rain, snow, wind and cold. Some of the feathers act as cloaks or mackintoshes and others as underclothing.

Method— The hen should be at close range for this lesson where the children may observe how and where the different kinds of feathers grow. The pupils should also study separately the form of a feather from the back, from the breast, from the under side of the body, and a pin-feather.

Pelicans are born naked, but are soon covered with white down.

Observations—

1. How are the feathers arranged on the back of the hen? Are they like shingles on the roof? If so, what for?

2. How does a hen look when standing in the rain?

3. How are the feathers arranged on the breast?

4. Compare a feather from the back and one from the breast and note the difference.

5. Are both ends of these feathers alike? If not, what is the difference?

6. Is the fluffy part of the feather on the outside or next to the bird's skin? What is its use?

7. Why is the smooth part of the feather (the web) on the outside?

8. Some feathers are all fluff and are called "down." At what age was the fowl all covered with down?

9. What is a pin-feather? What makes you think so?

10. How do hens keep their feathers oily and glossy so they will shed water?

11. Where does the hen get the oil? Describe how she oils her feathers and which ones does she oil most? Does she oil her feathers before a rain?

> "How beautiful your feathers be!"
> The Redbird sang to the Tulip-tree
> New garbed in autumn gold.
> "Alas!" the bending branches sighed,
> "They cannot like your leaves abide
> To keep us from the cold!"
>
> —JOHN B. TABB.

Not a candidate for a beauty contest...
Look at the pin feathers!

Feathers as Ornament

TEACHER'S STORY

THE ornamental plumage of birds is one of the principal illustrations of a great principle of evolution. The theory is that the male birds win their mates because of their beauty, those that are not beautiful being doomed to live single and leave no progeny to inherit their dullness. On the other hand, the successful wooer hands down his beauty to his sons. However, another quite different principle acts upon the coloring of the plumage of the mother birds; for if they should develop bright colors themselves, they would attract the eyes of the enemy to their precious hidden nests; only by being inconspicuous, are they able to protect their eggs and nestlings from discovery and death. The mother partridge, for instance, is so nearly the color of the dead leaves

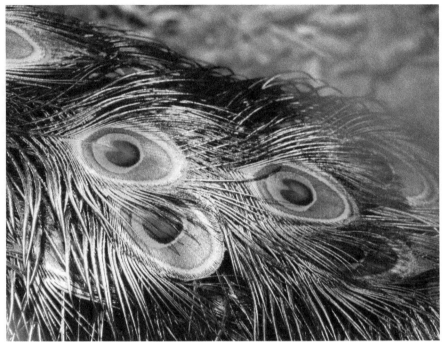

Peacock feathers. Is beauty useful?

on the ground about her, that we may almost step upon her before we discover her; if she were the color of the oriole or tanager she would very soon be the center of attraction to every prowler. Thus, it has come about that among the birds the feminine love of beauty has developed the gorgeous colors of the males, while the need for protection of the home has kept the female plumage modest and unnoticeable.

The curved feathers of the rooster's tail are weak and mobile and could not possibly be of any use as a rudder; but they give grace and beauty to the fowl and cover the useful rudder feathers underneath by a feather fountain of iridescence. The neck plumage of the cock is also often luxurious and beautiful in color and quite different from that of the hen. Among the ducks the brilliant blue-green iridescent head of the drake and his wing bars are beautiful, and make his wife seem Quaker-like in contrast.

As an object lesson to instil the idea that the male bird is proud of his beautiful feathers, I know of none better than that presented by the turkey gobbler, for he is a living expression of self-conscious

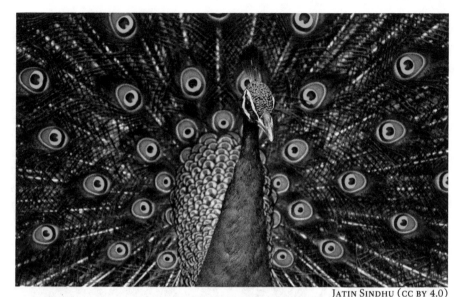

A peacock showing off its colors

vanity. He spreads his tail to the fullest extent and shifts it this way and that to show the exquisite play of colors over the feathers in the sunlight, meanwhile throwing out his chest to call particular attention to his blue and red wattles; and to keep from bursting with pride he bubbles over in vainglorious "gobbles."

The hen with her chicks and the turkey hen with her brood, if they follow their own natures, must wander in the fields for food. If they were bright in color, the hawks would soon detect them and their chances of escape would be small; this is another instance of the advantage to the young of adopting the colors of the mother rather than of the father; a fact equally true of the song birds in cases where the males are brilliant in color at maturity. The Baltimore oriole does not assist his mate in brooding, but he sits somewhere on the home tree and cheers her by his glorious song and by glimpses of his gleaming orange coat. Some have accused him of being lazy; on the contrary, he is a wise householder for, instead of attracting the attention of crow or squirrel to his nest, he distracts their attention from it by both color and song.

A peacock's feather should really be a lesson by itself, it is so much a thing of beauty. The brilliant color of the purple eye-spot, and the graceful flowing barbs that form the setting to the central gem, are all a training in aesthetics as well as in nature-study. After the children have studied such a feather let them see the peacock either in reality or in picture and give them stories about this bird of Juno; a bird so inconspicuous if it were not for his great spread of tail, that a child seeing it first cried, "Oh, oh, see this old hen all in bloom!"

The whole question of sexual selection may be made as plain as need be for the little folks, by simply telling them that the mother bird chooses for her mate the one which is most brightly and beautifully dressed, and make much of the comb and wattles of the rooster and gobbler as additions to the brilliancy of their appearance.

LESSON

Leading thought— The color of feathers and often their shape are for the purpose of making birds more beautiful; while in others, the color of the feathers protects them from the observation of their enemies.

Methods— While parts of this lesson relating to fowls, may be given in primary grades, it is equally fitted for pupils who have a wider knowledge of birds. Begin with a comparison of the plumage of the hen and the rooster. Then, if possible, study the turkey gobbler and a peacock in life or in pictures. Also the plumage of a Rouen duck and drake, and if possible, the Baltimore oriole, the goldfinch, the scarlet tanager and the cardinal.

Observations—

1. Note difference in shape and color of the tail feathers of hen and rooster.

2. Do the graceful curved tail feathers of the rooster help him in flying? Are they stiff enough to act as a rudder?

3. If not of use in flying what are they for? Which do you think the more beautiful: the hen or the rooster?

4. In what respects is the rooster a more beautiful fowl?

5. What other parts of the rooster's plumage is more beautiful than that of the hen?

6. If a turkey gobbler sees you looking at him he begins to strut. Do you think he does this to show off his tail feathers? Note how he turns his spread tail this way and that so the sunshine will bring out

the beautiful changeable colors. Do you think he does this so you can see and admire him?

7. Describe the difference in plumage between the hen turkey and the gobbler. Does the hen turkey strut?

8. Note the beautiful blue-green iridescent head and wing patches on the wings of the Rouen ducks. Is the drake more beautiful than the duck?

9. What advantage is it for these fowls to have the father bird more beautiful and bright in color than the mother bird?

10. In case of the Baltimore oriole is the mother bird as bright in color as the father bird? Why?

11. Study a peacock's feather. What color is the eye-spot? What color around that? What color and shape are the outside barbs of the feather? Do you blame a peacock for being proud when he can spread a tail of a hundred eyes? Does the peahen have such beautiful tail feathers as the peacock?

> *The bird of Juno glories in his plumes;*
> *Pride makes the fowl to preene his feathers so.*
> *His spotted train fetched from old Argus' head,*
> *With golden rays like to the brightest sun,*
> *Inserteth self-love in the silly bird;*
> *Till midst its hot and glorious fumes*
> *He spies his feet and then lets fall his plumes.*
> —"THE PEACOCK", ROBERT GREENE (1560).

Common tern. While we are having winter this bird spends the summer in South America. It will return to spend our summer with us

How Birds Fly

TEACHER'S STORY

TO convince the children that a bird's wings correspond to our arms, they should see a fowl with its feathers off, prepared for market or oven, and they will infer the fact at once.

The bird flies by lifting itself through pressing down upon the air with its wings. There are several experiments which are needed to make the child understand this. It is difficult for children to conceive that the air is really anything, because they cannot see it; so the first experiment should be to show that the air is something we can push against or that pushes against us. Strike the air with a fan and we feel there is something which the fan pushes; we feel the wind when it is blowing and it is very difficult for us to walk against a hard wind. If we hold an open umbrella in the hand while we jump from a step we feel buoyed up because the umbrella presses down upon the air. The bird presses down upon the air with the wings, just as the open umbrella does. The bird flies by pressing down upon the air with its wings just as a boy jumps high by pressing down with his hands on his vaulting pole.

Study wing and note: (a) That the wings open and close at the will of the bird. (b) That the feathers open and shut on each other like a fan. (c) When the wing is open the wing quills overlap, so that the air cannot pass through them. (d) When the wing is open it is curved so that it is more efficient, for the same reason that an umbrella presses harder against the atmosphere when it is open than when it is broken by the wind and turned wrong side out.

A hens wing outstretched showing primaries and secondaries of the wing and the overlapping of the feathers.

A wing feather has the barbs on the front edge lying almost parallel to the quill while those on the hind edge come off at a wide angle. The reason for this is easy to see, for this feather has to cut the air as the bird flies; and if the barbs on the front side were like those of the other side they would be torn apart by the wind. The barbs on the hind side of the feather form a strong, close web so as to press down on the air and not let it through. The wing quill is curved; the convex side is up and the concave side below during flight. The concave side, like the umbrella, catches more air than the upper side; the down stroke of the wing is forward and down; while on the up stroke, as the wing is lifted, it bends at the joint like a fan turned sidewise, and offers less surface to resist the air. Thus, the up stroke does not push the bird down.

Observations should be made on the use of the bird's tail in flight. The hen spreads her tail like a fan when she flies to the top of the fence; the robin does likewise when in flight. The fact that the tail is used as a rudder to guide the bird in flight, as well as to give more surface for pressing down upon the air, is hard for the younger pupils to understand, and perhaps can be best taught by watching the erratic unbalanced flight of young birds whose tail feathers are not yet grown.

The tail feather differs from the wing feather in that the quill is not curved, and the barbs on each side are of about equal length and lie at about the same angle on each side the quill.

References— The Bird Book, Eckstorm, pp. 75-92; Story of the Birds, Baskett, pp. 171-176; Bird Life, Chapman, p. 18; The Bird, Beebe, Ch. XIII; First Book of Birds, Miller.

LESSON

Leading thought— A bird flies by pressing down upon the air with its wings, which are made especially for this purpose. The bird's tail acts as a rudder during flight.

Method— The hen, it is hoped, will by this time be tame enough so that the teacher may spread open her wings for the children to see. In addition, have a detached wing of a fowl such as are used in farm houses instead of a whisk-broom.

Observations—

1. Do you think a bird's wings correspond to our arms? If so why?

2. Why do birds flap their wings when they start to fly?

3. Can you press against the air with a fan?

4. Why do you jump so high with a vaulting pole? Do you think the bird uses the air as you use the pole?

5. How are the feathers arranged on the wing so that the bird can use it to press down on the air?

6. If you carry an umbrella on a windy morning, which catches more wind, the under or the top side? Why is this? Does the curved surface of the wing act in the same way?

7. Take a wing feather. Are the barbs as long on one side of the quill as on the other? Do they lie at the same angle from the quill on both sides? If not why?

8. Which side of the quill lies on the outer side and which on the inner side of the wing?

9. Is the quill of the feather curved?

10. Which side is uppermost in the wing, the convex or the concave side? Take a quill in one hand and press the tip against the other. Which way does it bend easiest, toward the convex or the concave side? What has this to do with the flight of the bird?

11. If the bird flies by pressing the wings against the air on the down stroke, why does it not push itself downward with its wings on the up stroke?

12. What is the shape and arrangement of the feathers so as to avoid pushing the bird back to earth when it lifts its wings?

13. Why do you have a rudder to a boat?

14. Do you think a bird could sail through the air without something to steer with? What is the bird's rudder?

15. Have you ever seen a young bird whose tail is not yet grown, try to fly? If so, how did it act?

16. Does the hen when she flies keep the tail closed or open like a fan?

17. Compare a tail feather with a wing feather and describe the difference.

Migration of Birds

The travelogues of birds are as fascinating as our favorite stories of fairies, ad venture, and fiction. If we could accompany certain birds, such as the Arctic terns, on their spring and autumn trips, the logs of the trips would be far more ex citing than some recorded by famous aviators. The Arctic tern seems to hold the record for long-distance flight. Its nest is made within the bounds of the Arctic circle and its winter home is in the region of the Antarctic circle. The round-trip mile age for this bird during a year is about 22,000 miles. Wells W. Cooke, a pioneer student of bird migration, has called attention to the interesting fact that the Arctic tern "has more hours of daylight than any other animal on the globe. At the northern nesting-site the midnight sun has already appeared before the birds' arrival, and it never sets during their entire stay at the breeding grounds. During two months of their sojourn in the Antarctic the birds do not see a sunset, and for the rest of the time the sun dips only a little way below the horizon and broad day light is continuous. The birds, therefore, have twenty-four hours of daylight for at least eight months in the year, and during the other four months have considerably more daylight than darkness." It is true that few of our birds take such long trips as does the Arctic tern; but most birds do travel for some distance each spring and fall.

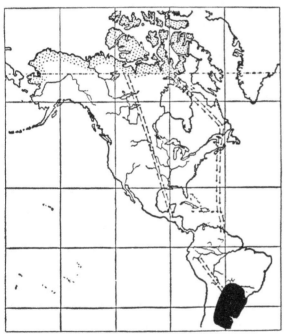

The migration routes of the golden plover. The dotted area is the summer home and nesting place ; the black area is the winter home. Migration routes are indicated by arrows. On the southern route the plover makes a flight of 2,400 miles from Labrador to South America

Each season brings to our attention certain changes in the bird population. During late summer, we see great flocks of swallows; they are on telephone or telegraph wires, wire fences, clothes lines, or aerial wires. They twitter and flutter and seem all excited. For a few days, as they prepare for their southern journey, they are seen in such groups, and then are seen no more until the following spring. Some birds do not gather in flocks before leaving for the winter; they just disappear: and we scarcely know when they go. We may hear their call notes far over our heads as they wing their way to their winter homes. Some birds migrate only during the day, others go only during the night, and others may travel by either day or night. Those birds that do not migrate are called permanent residents. In the east ern United States chickadees, jays, downy woodpeckers, nuthatches, grouse, and pheasants are typical examples of the permanent resident group. These birds must be able to secure food under even the most adverse conditions. Much of their food is insect life found in or about trees; some fruits and buds of trees, shrubs, and vines are also included in their diet.

Birds that travel are called migratory birds. If the spring migrants remain with us for the summer, we call them our sun mer residents. Fall migrants that remain with us for the winter are called winter residents. The migrants that do not re main with us but pass on to spend the summer or winter in some other area are called our transients or visitors. Of course, we must remember that the birds which visit us only for a short time are summer residents and winter residents in other parts of the country. Our summer residents are the winter residents of some other area.

In spring we await with interest the arrival of the first migrants. These birds are, in general, those which have spent the winter only a comparatively short distance away. In the eastern United States, we expect robins, red-winged blackbirds, song sparrows, and bluebirds among the earliest migrants. In many species the males arrive first; they may come as much as two weeks ahead of the females. The immature birds are usually the last to arrive. The time of arrival of the first migrants is determined somewhat by weather conditions; their dates cannot be predicted with as much accuracy as can those of birds

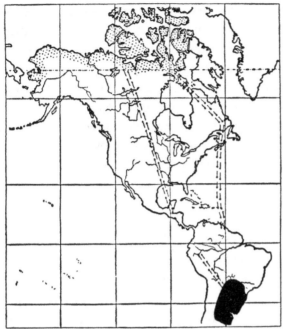

The travels of the bobolink. The migration routes of the bobolink are shorter than those of the plover and follow land more closely

which, having spent the winter at a greater distance from us, arrive later when the weather is more favorable. In some places, for example at Ithaca, New York, bird records have been kept each season for more than thirty years. With the information from these records, it is possible to indicate almost to a day when certain birds, such as barn swallows, orioles, or hummingbirds, may be expected to arrive. Usually the very first birds of a kind to arrive are those individuals which will within a few days continue their northward journey. The later arrivals are usually those that remain to become sum mer residents. In some species all individuals are migrants; for southern New York the white-throated sparrow is representative of such a group. It winters far the south and nests farther north than southern New York.

Why do birds migrate? This question has often been asked; but in answer to it we must say that while we know much about where birds go and how fast they travel, we still know actually very little about the reasons for their regular seasonal journeys.

As the airplane pilot has man-made in instruments to aid him in reaching a certain airport, so the birds have a well-developed sense of direction which guides them to their destination. Each kind of bird seems, in general, to take the route followed by its ancestors; but this route may be varied if for any reason food should become scarce along the way. Such routes are so exactly followed year after year that they are known as lanes of migration. Persons desiring to study a certain species of bird can have excellent op opportunities to do so by being at some good vantage point along this lane. Some times undue advantage has been taken of certain birds, especially hawks. Persons desiring to kill these birds have collected at strategic points along the lanes and wantonly killed many of them. As a result of such activities sanctuaries have been established at certain places along the lanes to give added protection to birds. The routes north and south followed by a given species of bird may lead over entirely different parts of the country; these are called double migration routes. They may vary so much that one route may lead chiefly over land while the other may lead over the ocean. The golden plover is an example of such a case. See the migration map.

Much valuable information as well as pleasure can be gained from keeping a calendar of migration and other activities of birds. It is especially interesting during the spring months when first arrivals are recorded if daily lists are made of all species observed. In summer, nesting ac activities and special studies of an individual species provide something of interest for each day. More pleasure can be derived from the hobby if several people take it up and compare their findings. Interests in photography, sketching, of nature-story writing are natural companions of such bird study.

SUGGESTED READING – *Bird Friends*, by - Gilbert H. Trafton; *Bird Life*, by Frank M. Chapman; *Birds and Their Attributes*, by Glover M. Allen; *Birds of America*, edited by T. Gilbert Pearson; *Birds of New York*, by E. H. Eaton; *The Book of Bird Life*, by A. A. Allen; *The Book of Birds*, edited by Gilbert Grosvenor and Alexander Wetmore; *The Children's Book of Birds* (First Book of Birds and Second Book of Birds), by Olive Thorne Miller; *Flight Speed of Birds*, by May Thacher Cooke (U. S. Department of Agriculture, Circular 428); *The Migration of North American Birds*, by Frederick C. Lincoln (U. S. Department of Agriculture, Circular 363); *Nature—by Seaside and Wayside*, by Mary G. Phillips and Julia M. Wright, Book 3, *Plants and Animals; Our Winter Birds*, by Frank M. Chapman; *Pathways in Science*, by Gerald S. Craig and Co-authors, Book 2, *Out-of-doors*, Book 5, *Learning about Our World; The Stir of Nature*, by William H. Carr; *Traveling with the Birds*, by Rudyerd Boulton; *The Travels of Birds*, by Frank M. Chapman.

A Saker Falcon. Notice the strong hooked beak, the keen eye, and the prominent nostril.

Eyes and Ears of Birds

TEACHER'S STORY

THE hen's eyes are placed at the side of the head so that she cannot see the same object with both eyes at the same time, and thus she has the habit of looking at us first with one eye and then the other to be sure she sees correctly; also the position of the hen's eyes give her a command of her entire environment. All birds have much keener eyes than have we; and they can adjust their eyes for either near or far vision much more effectively than we can; the hawk, flying high in the air, can see the mouse on the ground.

There is a wide range of colors found in the eyes of birds; white, red, blue, yellow, brown, gray, pink, purple and green are found in the iris of different species. The hen's eye consists of a black pupil at the center, which must always be black in any eye, since it is a hole through which enters the image of the object. The iris of the hen's eye is yellow; there is apparently no upper lid but the lower lid comes up during the process of sleeping. When the bird is drowsy the little film lid comes out from the corner of the eye and spreads over it like a veil; just at the corner of our own eye, next the nose, is the remains of this film lid, although we cannot move it as the hen does.

The hearing of birds is very acute, although the ear is simply a hole in the side of the head in most cases, and is more or less covered with feathers. The hen's ear is like this in many varieties; but in others and in the roosters there are ornamental ear lobes.

Lesson

Leading thought— The eyes and ears of birds are peculiar and very efficient.

Methods— The hen or chicken and the rooster should be observed for this lesson; notes may be made in the poultry yard or in the schoolroom when the birds are brought there for study.

Observations—

1. Why does the hen turn her head first this side and that as she looks at you? Can she see an object with both eyes at once? Can she see well?

2. How many colors are there in a hen's eye? Describe the pupil and the iris.

3. Does the hen wink as we do? Has she any eyelids?

4. Can you see the film lid? Does it come from above or below or the inner or outer corner? When do you see this film lid?

5. Where are the hen's ears? How do they look? How can you tell where the rooster's ears are?

6. Do you think the hen can see and hear well?

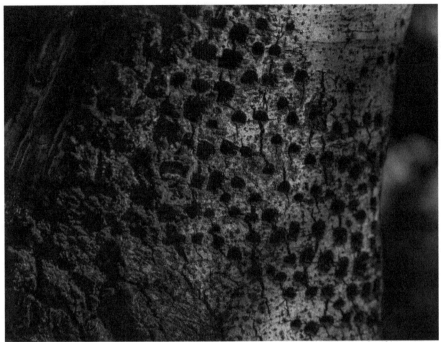
Woodpecker holes in a tree. These were made by a woodpecker in search of insects

The Form and Use of Beaks

TEACHER'S STORY

SINCE the bird uses its arms and hands for flying, it has been obliged to develop other organs to take their place, and of their work the beak does its full share. It is well to emphasize this point by letting the children at recess play the game of trying to eat an apple or to put up their books and pencils with their arms tied behind them; such an experiment will show how naturally the teeth and feet come to the aid when the hands are useless.

The hen feeds upon seeds and insects which she finds on or in the ground; her beak is horny and sharp and acts not only as a pair of nippers, but also as a pick as she strikes it into the soil to get the seed or insect, having already made bare the place by scratching away the grass or surface of the soil with her strong, stubby toes. The hen does not have any teeth, nor does she need any, for her sharp beak enables her to seize her food; and she does not need to chew it, since her gizzard does this for her after the food is swallowed.

The duck's bill is broad, flat, and much softer than the hen's beak. The duck feeds upon water insects and plants; it attains these by thrusting its head down into the water, seizing the food and holding it fast while the water is strained out through the sieve at the edges of the beak; for this use, a wide, flat beak is necessary. It would be quite as impossible for a duck to pick up hard seeds with its broad, soft bill as it would for the hen to get the duck's food out of the water with her narrow, horny bill.

Both the duck and hen use their bills for cleaning and oiling their feathers and for fighting also; the hen strikes a sharp blow with her beak making a wound like a dagger, while the duck seizes the enemy and simply pinches hard. Both fowls also use their beaks for turning over the eggs when incubating, and also as an aid to the feet when they make nests for themselves.

The nostrils are very noticeable and are situated in the beak near the base. However, we do not believe that birds have a keen sense of smell since their nostrils are not surrounded by a damp, sensitive, soft

Black-headed weaver (Ploceus cucullatus bohndorffi) *male building a nest*

surface as are the nostrils of the deer and dog, this arrangement aiding these animals to detect odor in a marvelous manner.

LESSON

Leading thought— Each kind of bird has a beak especially adapted for getting its food. The beak and feet of a bird are its chief weapons and implements.

Methods— Study first the beak of the hen or chick and then that of the duckling or gosling.

Observations—

1. What kind of food does the hen eat and where and how does she find it in the field or garden? How is her beak adapted to get this food? If her beak were soft like that of a duck could she peck so hard for seeds and worms? Has the hen any teeth? Does she need any?

2. Compare the bill of the hen with that of the duck. What are the differences in shape? Which is the harder?

3. Note the saw teeth along the edge of the duck's bill. Are these for chewing? Do they act as a strainer? Why does the duck need to strain its food?

4. Could a duck pick up a hen's food from the earth or the hen strain out a duck's food from the water? For what other things than getting food do these fowls use their bills?

5. Can you see the nostrils in the bill of a hen? Do they show plainer in the duck? Do you think the hen can smell as keenly as the duck?

Supplementary reading— *The Bird Book*, p. 99; *The First Book of Birds*, pp. 95-7; *Mother Nature's Children*, Chapter VIII.

"It is said that nature-study teaching should be accurate, a statement that every good teacher will admit without debate; but accuracy is often interpreted to mean completeness, and then the statement cannot pass unchallenged. To study 'the dandelion,' 'the robin,' with emphasis on the article 'the,' working out the complete structure, may be good laboratory work in botany or zoology for advanced pupils, but it is not an elementary educational process. It contributes nothing more to accuracy than does the natural order of leaving untouched all

those phases of the subject that are out of the child's reach; while it may take out the life and spirit of the work, and the spiritual quality may be the very part that is most worth the while. Other work may provide the formal 'drill'; this should supply the quality and vivacity. Teachers often say to me that their children have done excellent work with these complete methods, and they show me the essays and drawings; but this is no proof that the work is commendable. Children can be made to do many things that they ought not to do and that lie beyond them. We all need to go to school to children."

—"THE OUTLOOK TO NATURE," L. H. BAILEY.

"Weather and wind and waning moon,
Plain and hilltop under the sky,
Ev'ning, morning and blazing noon,
Brother of all the world am I.
The pine-tree, linden and the maize,
The insect, squirrel and the kine,
All—natively they live their days—
As they live theirs, so I live mine,
I know not where, I know not what:—
Believing none and doubting none
What'er befalls it counteth not,—
Nature and Time and I are one."

—L. H. BAILEY.

A close-up of a White Cockatoo's feet

The Feet of Birds

TEACHER'S STORY

OBVIOUSLY, the hen is a digger of the soil; her claws are long, strong and slightly hooked, and her feet and legs are covered with horny scales as a protection from injury when used in scratching the hard earth, in order to lay bare the seeds and insects hiding there. The hen is a very good runner indeed. She lifts her wings a little to help, much as an athletic runner uses his arms, and so can cover ground with amazing rapidity, her strong toes giving her a firm foothold. The track she makes is very characteristic; it consists of three toe-marks projecting forward and one backward. A bird's toes are numbered thus:

A duck has the same number of toes as the hen, but there is a membrane, called the web, which joins the second, third and fourth toes, making a fan-shaped foot; the first or the hind toe has a little web of its own. A webbed foot is first of all a paddle for propelling its owner through the water; it is also a very useful foot on the shores of ponds and streams, since its breadth and flatness prevent it from sinking into the soft mud.

Duck's foot and hen's foot with toes numbered.

The duck's legs are shorter than those of the hen and are placed farther back and wider apart. The reason for this is, they are essentially swimming organs and are not fitted for scratching nor for running. They are placed at the sides of the bird's body so that they may act as paddles, and are farther back so that they may act like the wheel of a propeller in pushing the bird along. We often laugh at a duck on land, since its short legs are so far apart and so far back that its walk is necessarily an awkward waddle; but we must always remember that the duck is naturally a water bird, and on the water its movements are graceful. Think once, how a hen would appear if she attempted to swim! The duck's body is so illy balanced on its short legs that it cannot run rapidly; and if chased even a short distance, will fall dead from the effort, as many a country child has discovered to his sorrow when he tried to drive the ducks home from the creek or pond to coop. The long, hind claw of the hen enables her to clasp a roost firmly during the night; a duck's foot could not do this and the duck sleeps squatting on the ground. However, the Muscovy ducks, which are not good swimmers, have been known to perch.

LESSON

Leading thought— The feet of birds are shaped so as to assist the bird in getting its food as well as for locomotion.

Methods—The pupils should have opportunity to observe the chicken or hen and a duck as they move about; they should also observe the duck swimming.

Observations—

1. Are the toes of the hen long and strong? Have they long, sharp claws at their tips?

2. How are the legs and feet of the hen covered and protected?

3. How are the hen's feet and legs fitted for scratching the earth, and why does she wish to scratch the earth?

4. Can a hen run rapidly? What sort of a track does she make?

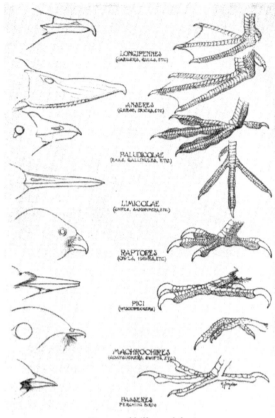

LONGIPENNES
(ALBATROSS, GULLS, ETC.)

ANSERES
(GEESE, DUCKS, ETC.)

PALUDICOLAE
(RAILS, GALLINULES, ETC.)

LIMICOLAE
(SNIPES, SANDPIPERS, ETC.)

RAPTORES
(OWLS, HAWKS, ETC.)

PICI
(WOODPECKERS)

MACHROCHIRES
(HUMMINGBIRDS, SWIFTS, ETC.)

PASSERES
PERCHING BIRDS

Types of bills and feet

5. You number your fingers with the thumb as number one and the little finger as five. How do you think the hen's toes are numbered?

6. Has the duck as many toes as the hen? What is the chief difference between the feet of the duck and the hen?

7. Which of the duck's toes are connected by a web? Does the web extend to the tips of the toes? What is the web for and how does it help the duck?

8. Are the duck's legs as long as the hen's? Are they placed farther forward or farther back than those of the hen? Are they farther apart?

9. Can a duck run as well as a hen? Can the hen swim at all?

10. Where does the hen sleep and how does she hold on to her perch? Could the duck hold on to a perch? Does the duck need to perch while sleeping?

Songs of Birds

Anyone who attempts to recognize birds by sight alone misses much of the pleasure that comes to those who have taken the time and pains to learn bird songs and use them as a means of bird recognition. It is true that not all people have a talent for music; but anyone interested in birds can learn to identify the songs and most of the call notes of common birds.

The observer will notice that in most cases only the male bird sings, but a few exceptions are recorded, notably the female rose-breasted grosbeak and cardinal grosbeak, which sing under some conditions. Birds do most of their singing in the early morning and during the spring and early summer months. The male birds have not only a favorite time of day and a particular season of the year during which they do most of their singing, but they even have a certain perch or narrowly defined territory from which they sing.

Each person will need to decide how he can best remember bird songs. Most people will doubtless use such methods as were used by earlier bird students. Long literary descriptions were given for each song. Alexander Wilson, for instance, describes the call of the male blue jay as "repeated creakings of an ungreased wheelbarrow." Often the call of a particular bird is put into words; in many cases these words have come to be accepted as the common name of the bird, such as bobwhite and whip-poor-will. The imagination of students may

Notations.

suggest certain words to represent the song or call notes of a bird. These are often more easily remembered than the song itself.

Some ornithologists have developed complicated systems of recording bird songs as musical scores. Wilson Flagg and F. S. Mathews are well-known names in this field. Such a method has its limitations because many variations of bird songs cannot be indicated by the characters used in writing music. The song of a bird written as music is not usually recognizable when played on a musical instrument. Other ornithologists have developed more graphic methods of recording bird songs. One leader in this field, A. A. Saunders, has proposed and used a system employing lines, dots, dashes, and syllables. This system is very interesting and is a useful one to a person who has a good ear for music. One of the latest methods of recording bird songs has been developed by the Department of Ornithology, Cornell University, Ithaca, New York. By this method bird songs are photographed on moving picture film and later may be recorded on phonograph records; these records can be played over and over again to give the student practice in identifying bird songs. Sound pictures have also been produced; the pictures of the various birds are shown on the screen as their songs are being heard by the audience.

SUGGESTED READING - *Bird Friends*, by Gilbert H. Trafton; *Birds and Their Attributes*, by Glover M. Allen; *The Book of Bird Life*, by A. A. Allen;

The Book of Birds, edited by Gilbert Grosvenor and Alexander Wetmore; *Field Book of Wild Birds and Their Music*, by F. Schuyler Mathews; *A Guide to Bird Songs*, by Aretas A. Saunders; *Songs of Wild Birds and More Songs of Wild Birds*, by Albert R. Brand.

A Robin singing

Blue Jays In a Bird Bath

Attracting Birds

If suitable and sufficient food, water, shelter, and nesting sites are provided, and if protection is given from such enemies as cats and thoughtless men, it is possible to attract many kinds of birds to home grounds or gardens. The most logical time to begin to attract birds is during the winter months; but the best time is whenever one is really interested and is willing to provide the things most needed by the birds. Certain types of food, such as suet or sunflower seeds, are sought by birds at any season. During the summer months water for drinking and bathing may be more desired than food, but in the winter almost any seeds, fruits, or fatty foods are welcome.

In the spring nesting boxes properly constructed and placed will do much to attract some kinds of birds, especially those that normally nest in holes in trees. An abundance of choice nesting materials will entice orioles, robins, or chipping sparrows to nest nearby. Straws, sticks, feathers, cotton, strings, or even hairs from old mattresses may be put out as inducements to prospective bird tenants. The spring is also a good time to plant fruit-bearing trees, shrubs, and vines; these natural food counters become more attractive each year as they grow larger and produce more fruit and better nesting places for birds.

Autumn is the ideal time to establish feeding centers to which the birds may be attracted during the winter months. Food, such as suet or seeds, should be put at a great many places throughout the area in which one wishes to attract birds. The birds will gradually work their way from one of these feedings points to another; soon it will be possible to concentrate the feeding at one point, and the birds will continue to come to that point as long as food is provided there.

SUGGESTED READING - *The A B C of Attracting Birds*, by Alvin M. Peterson; *Bird Houses Boys Can Build*, by Albert F. Siepert; *Birds of the Wild - How to Make Your Home Their Home*, by Frank C. Pellett; *Bird Study for Schools Series*, published by the National Association of Audubon Societies (Part III, Winter Feeding, Part IV, Bird Houses); *The Book of Bird Life*, by A. A. Allen; *Boy Bird House Architecture*, by Leon H. Baxter; *The Children's Book of Birds* (First Book of Birds and Second Book of Birds), by Olive Thorne Miller; *Homes for Birds*, by E. R. Kalmbach and W. L. McAtee (U. S. Department of Agriculture, Farmers' Bulletin 1456); *How to Attract Birds in Northeastern United States, How to Attract Birds in Northwestern United States, How to Attract Birds in the Middle Atlantic States, How to Attract Birds in the East Central States*, by W. L. McAtee (U. S. Department of Agriculture, Farmers' Bulletins 621, 760, 844,912); *How to Have Bird Neighbors*, by S. Louise Patteson; *Our Winter Birds*, by Frank M. Chapman; *Permanent Bird Houses*, by Gladstone Califf; *Song-bird Sanctuaries, with Tables of Trees, Shrubs and Vines Attractive to Birds*, by Roger T. Peterson; *Wild Bird Guests*, by Ernest H. Baynes; *Methods of Attracting Birds*, by Gilbert H. Trafton.

Warbling Vireo (Vireo gilvus) *on nest. Vireos live largely on insects gleaned from the under surfaces of leaves and from crevices in bark*

Value of Birds

Did you ever try to calculate in dollars the pleasure that you receive from seeing or hearing the first spring migrants? The robin, bluebird, and meadowlark bring cheer to thousands of people every year. Indeed, it would be difficult to find anyone, except perhaps in large cities, who does not notice the arrival of at least some spring birds—the robins on the lawn, the honk of the wild geese overhead, or the song sparrows as they sing from the top of a shrub. Birds are interesting to most people because of their mere presence, their songs, their colors, or their habits. Persons engaged in nature-study are led outdoors and thus have opened to them many other nature fields.

One needs to observe a bird for only a short time to discover for himself what has been known by scientists for many years, that birds are of great economic importance. Watch a chickadee or nuthatch as it makes its feeding rounds on a winter day. Note how carefully each tiny branch is covered by the chickadee and what a thorough examination of the limbs and trunks is made by the nuthatch. Countless insect eggs as well as insects are consumed. On a sunny day in spring, observe the warblers as they feed about the newly opened leaves and blossoms of the trees. See them as they hunt tirelessly for their quota of the tiny insects so small that they are generally overlooked by larger birds. It must be remembered too that some birds do, at times, take a toll of cultivated crops; this is especially true of the seed-eating and insectivorous birds. But they deserve some pay for the work they do for man, and so in reality he should not begrudge them a little fruit or grain.

Some of the birds of prey are active all the time; the hawks work in the daytime and the owls come on duty for the night shift. Countless destructive small mammals and insects are eaten by them; thus they tend to regulate the numbers of numerous small pests of field and wood, thereby preventing serious outbreaks of such animals. There has been much discussion of the real economic status of hawks and owls; many food studies have been made and the general conclusion is that most species are more useful than harmful. It is true that some species do take a toll of game birds, song birds, and poultry; but they include also in their diet other animal forms, many of which are considered harm-

A winter bird nest with snow

A bluebird outside a birdhouse

ful. One individual bird may be especially destructive and thus give a bad name to an entire species.

There are even garbage gatherers among the birds; vultures, gulls, and crows serve in this capacity. The vultures are commonly found in the warmer parts of the country and serve a most useful purpose by their habit of devouring the unburied bodies of dead animals. The gulls are the scavengers of waterways and shore lines. The crow is omnivorous - that is, it eats both plant and animal food; but it seems to like carrion as well as fresh meat.

The farmer and the gardener owe quite a debt of thanks to the birds that eat weed seeds. Of course there are still bountiful crops of weeds each year; but there would be even more weeds if it were not for the army of such seed-eating birds as sparrows, bobwhites, and doves.

The game birds, such as grouse, pheasant, and bobwhite are important today, chiefly from the standpoint of the recreation they afford sportsmen and other lovers of the outdoors. The food habits of game birds do not present much of an economic problem; the birds are not numerous enough at the present time to be an important source of meat for man as they were in pioneer days.

Thus, a brief consideration of a few types of birds will show even

Hummingbird at feeder

a casual observer that birds have economic importance and that each species seems to have a definite work to perform.

SUGGESTED READING - *Bird Friends,* by Gilbert H. Trafton; *Birds and Their At tributes,* by Glover M. Allen; *Birds in Their Relation to Man,* by Clarence M. Weed and Ned Dearborn; *The Book of Bird Life,* by A. A. Allen; *The Book of Birds,* edited by Gilbert Grosvenor and Alexander Wetmore; *The Children's Book of Birds (First Book of Birds and Second Book of Birds),* by Olive Thorne Miller; *The Practical Value of Birds,* by Junius Henderson.

LESSON

There are very good reasons for not studying birds' nests in summer, since the birds misinterpret familiarity on the part of eager children and are likely, in consequence, to abandon both nest and locality. But after the birds have gone to sunnier climes and the empty nests are the only mementos we have of them, then we may study these habitations carefully and learn how to appreciate properly the small architects which made them. I think that every one of us who carefully examines the way that a nest is made must have a feeling of respect for its clever little builder.

I know of certain schools where the children make large collections of these winter nests, properly labeling each, and thus gain a new interest in the bird life of their locality. A nest when collected should be labeled in the following manner:

The name of the bird which built the nest.

Where the nest was found. If in a tree, what kind?

How high from the ground?

After a collection of nests has been made, let the pupils study them according to the following outline:

1. Where was the nest found?

    (a) If on the ground, describe the locality.

    (b) If on a plant, tree, or shrub, tell the species, if possible.

    (c) If on a tree, tell where it was on a branch—in a fork, or hanging by the end of the twigs.

    (d) How high from the ground, and what was the locality?

    (e) If on or in a building, how situated?

2. Did the nest have any arrangement to protect it from rain?

3. Give the size of the nest, the diameter of the inside and the outside; also the depth of the inside.

4. What is the form of the nest? Are its sides flaring or straight? Is the nest shaped like a cup, basket, or pocket?

5. What materials compose the outside of the nest and how are they arranged?

6. Of what materials is the lining made, and how are they arranged? If hair or feathers are used, on what creature did they grow?

7. How are the materials of the nest held together, that is, are they woven, plastered, or held in place by environment?

8. Had the nest anything peculiar about it either in situation, construction, or material that would tend to render it invisible to the casual glance?

SUGGESTED READING - *The Book of Bird Life*, by A. A. Allen; *Nature - by Seaside and Wayside*, by Mary G. Phillips and Julia M. Wright, *Book 3, Plants and Animals; Ornithology Laboratory Notebook*, by A. A. Allen; *A Year in the Wonderland of Birds*, by Hallam Hawksworth.

The Life History of Insects

NSECTS are among the most interesting and available of all living creatures for nature-study. The lives of many of them afford more interesting stories than are found in fairy lore; many of them show exquisite colors and, more than all, they are small and are, therefore, easily confined for observation.

While the young pupils should not be drilled in insect anatomy, as if they were embryo zoologists, yet it is necessary for the teacher, who would teach intelligently, to know something of the life stories, habits and structure of the common insects. Generally speaking, all insects develop from eggs. To most of us the word egg brings before us the picture of the egg of the hen or of some other bird. But insect eggs are often far more beautiful than those of any bird; they are of widely differing forms, and are often exquisitely colored and the shells may be ornately ribbed and pitted, sometimes adorned with spines, and are as beautiful to look at through a microscope as the most artistic piece of mosaic.

From the eggs, larvae (*sing. larva*) issue. These larvae may be cater-

The egg of the cotton moth, greatly enlarged.

pillars, or the creatures commonly called worms, or may be maggots or grubs. The larval stage is always devoted to feeding and to growth. It is the chief business of the larva to eat diligently and to attain maturity as soon as possible; for often the length of the larval period depends more upon food than upon lapse of time. All insects have their skeletons on the outside of the body; that is, the outer covering of the body is chitinous, and the soft and inner parts are attached to it and supported by it. This skin is so firm that it cannot stretch to accommodate the increasing size of the growing insect, thus from time to time it is shed. But before this is done, a new skin is formed beneath the old one. After the old skin bursts open and the insect crawls forth, the new skin is sufficiently soft and elastic to allow for the increase in the size of the insect. Soon, the new skin becomes hardened like the old

Caterpillar of the monarch butterfly

Butterfly chrysalis

one, and after a time, is shed. This shedding of the skin is called molting. Some insects shed their skins only four or five times during the period of attaining their growth, while other species may molt twenty times or more.

After the larva has attained its full growth, it changes its skin and its form, and becomes a pupa. The pupa stage is ordinarily one of inaction, except that very wonderful changes take place within the body itself. Usually the pupa has no power of moving around, but in many cases it can squirm somewhat, if disturbed. The pupa of the mosquito is active and is an exception to the rule. The pupa is usually an oblong object and seems to be without head, feet or wings; but if it is examined closely, especially in the case of butterflies and moths, the antennae, wings and legs may be seen, folded down beneath the pupa skin.

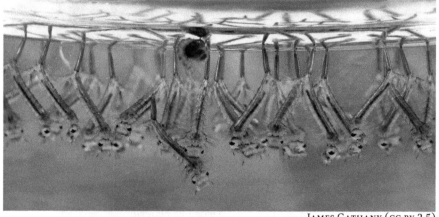
Mosquito larvae and one pupa, one of the only active pupa

A luna moth.

The delicate, exquisite green of the luna's wings is set off by the rose-purple, velvet border of the front wings, and the white for on the body and inner edge of the hind wings. Little wonder that it has been called the "Empress of the night". The long swallow tail of the hind wings give the moth a most graceful shape, at the same time probably afford it protection from observation. During the day time the moth hangs wings down beneath the green leaves, and these long projections of the hind wings folded together resemble a petiole, making the insect look very much like a large leaf

Many larvae, especially those of moths, weave about themselves a covering of silk which serves to protect them from their enemies and the weather, during the helpless pupa period. This silken covering is called a cocoon. The larvae of butterflies do not make a silken cocoon, but the pupa is suspended to some object by a silken knob, and in some cases by a halter of silk, and remains entirely naked. The pupa of a butterfly is called a chrysalis. Care should be taken to have the children

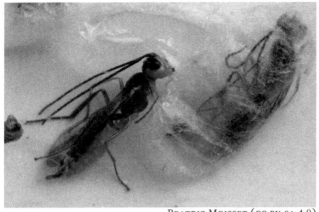

An adult Ichneumonid wasp emerging from a cocoon

use the words—pupa, chrysalis and cocoon—understandingly.

After a period varying from days to months, depending upon the species of insect and the climate, the pupa skin bursts open and from it emerges the adult insect, often equipped with large and beautiful wings and always provided with six legs and a far more complex structure of body than characterized it as a larva. The insect never grows after it reaches this adult stage and, therefore, never molts. Some people seem to believe that a small fly will grow into a large fly, and a small beetle into a large beetle; but after an insect attains its perfect wings, it does not grow larger. Many adult insects take very little food, although some continue to eat in order to support life. The adult stage is ordinarily shorter than the larval stage; it seems a part of nature's economic plan that the grown-up insects should live only long enough to lay eggs, and thus secure the continuation of the species. Insects having the four distinct stages in their growth, egg, larva, pupa and adult, are said to undergo complete metamorphosis.

But not all insects pass through an inactive pupa stage. With some insects, like the grasshoppers, the young, as soon as they are hatched, resemble the adult forms in appearance. These insects, like the larvae, shed their skins to accommodate their growth, but they continue to

A young grasshopper, enlarged.
The line shows its actual length

The adult of the same grasshopper,
natural size

feed and move about actively until the final molt when the perfect insect appears. Such insects are said to have incomplete metamorphosis, which simply means that the form of the body of the adult insect is not greatly different from that of the young; the dragon-flies, crickets, grasshoppers and bugs are of this type. The young of insects with an incomplete metamorphosis are called nymphs instead of larvae.

SUMMARY OF THE METAMORPHOSES OF INSECTS

Complete Metamorphosis
- Egg.
- Larva.
- Pupa. (The pupa is sometimes enclosed in a cocoon.)
- Adult or winged insect.

Incomplete Metamorphosis
- Egg.
- Nymph (several stages).
- Adult, or imago.

Insect brownies; tree-hoppers as seen through a lens

The Structure of Insects

THE insect body is made up of ring-like segments which are grown together. These segments are divided into groups according to their use and the organs which they bear. Thus the segments of an insect's body are grouped into three regions, the head, the thorax and the abdomen. The head bears the eyes, the antennae, and the mouth-parts. On each side of the head of the adult insect may be seen the compound eyes; these are so called, because they are made up of many small eyes set together, much like the cells of the honeycomb. These compound eyes are not found in larvae. In addition to the compound eyes, many adult insects possess simple eyes; these are placed between the compound eyes and are usually three in number. Often they cannot be seen without the aid of a lens.

The antennae or feelers are composed of many segments and are

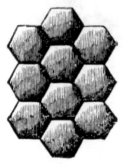

A part of the compound eye of an insect, enlarged

inserted in front of the eyes or between them. They vary greatly in form. In some insects they are mere threads; in others, like the silk-worm moths, they are large, feather-like organs.

The mouth-parts of insects vary greatly in structure and in form, being adapted to the life of the insect species to which they minister. Some insects have jaws fitted for seizing their prey, others for chewing leaves, others have a sucking tube for getting the juices from plants

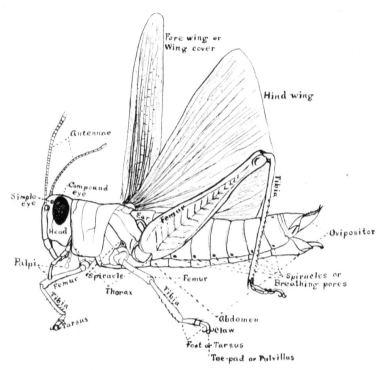

Grasshopper, with the parts of the external anatomy named

or the blood from animals, and others long delicate tubes for sipping the nectar from flowers.

In the biting insects, the mouth-parts consist of an upper lip, the labrum, and under lip, the labium, and two pairs of jaws between them. The upper pair of jaws is called the mandibles and the lower pair, the maxillae *(sing. maxilla)*. There may be also within the mouth, one or two tongue-like organs. Upon the maxillae and upon the lower lip there may also be feelers which are called palpi *(sing. palpus)*. The jaws of insects, when working, do not move up and down, as do ours, but move sidewise like shears. In many of the insects, the children are able to observe the mandibles and the palpi without the aid of a lens.

A tree hopper, showing the mouth as a long, three-jointed sucking tube, at a.

The thorax is the middle region of the insect body. It is composed of three of the body segments more or less firmly joined

85

together. The segment next the head is called the prothorax, the middle one, the mesothorax, and the hind one, the metathorax. Each of these segments bears a pair of legs and, in the winged insects, the second and third segments bear the wings. Each leg consists of two small segments next to the body, next to them a longer segment, called the femur, beyond this a segment called the tibia, and beyond this the tarsus or foot. The tarsus is made up of a number of segments, varying from one to six, the most common number being five. The last segment of the tarsus usually bears one or two claws.

Upper lip or labrum

Mandibles or Upper Jaws

Tongue

Palpus

Palpus

Maxillae or Lower Jaws.

Palpus

Palpus

Under lip or labram

The mouth-parts of a grasshopper dissected off, enlarged and named.

While we have little to do with the internal anatomy of insects in elementary nature-study, the children should be taught something of the way that insects breathe. The child naturally believes that the insect, like himself, breathes through the mouth, while as a matter of fact, insects breathe through their sides. If we examine almost any insect carefully, we can find along the sides of the body a series of openings. These are called the spiracles, and through them the air passes into the insect's body. The number of spiracles varies greatly in different insects. There is, however, never more than one pair on a single segment of the body, and they do

A sphinx moth using its with its tongue unrolled into a flower

not occur on the head. The spiracles, or breathing pores, lead into a system of air tubes which are called tracheae (tra'-ke-ee), which permeate the insect's body and thus carry the air to every smallest part of its anatomy. The blood of the insect bathes these thin-walled air tubes and thus becomes purified, just as our blood becomes purified by bathing the air tubes of our lungs. Thus, although the insects do not have localized breathing organs, like our lungs, they have, if the expression may be permitted, lungs in every part of their little bodies.

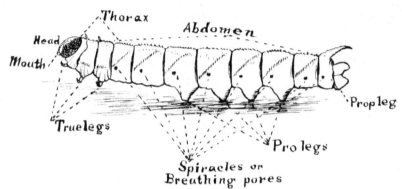

The sphinx caterpillar, with the parts of the external anatomy named

Head	Antennæ.		
	Compound eyes.		
	Simple eyes or ocelli.		
	Mouth-parts	Labrum, or upper lip.	
		Mandibles, or upper jaws.	
		Maxillæ, or lower jaws, and maxillary palpi.	
		Labium and labial palpi.	
Thorax	Prothorax and first pair of legs.		
	Mesothorax and	second pair of legs.	
		first pair of wings.	
	Metathorax and	third pair of legs.	
		second pair of wings.	
	Wing	veins.	
		cells.	
	Leg	Two small segments called coxa and trochanter.	
		Femur.	
		Tibia.	
		Tarsus and claws.	
Abdomen	The abdomen bears	ears (in locusts only).	
		spiracles.	
		ovipositor.	

White mountain laurel

How to Begin the Study of
Plants and Flowers

THE only right way to begin plant study with young children is through awakening their interest in and love for flowers. Most children love flowers naturally; they enjoy bringing flowers to school, and here, by teaching the recognition of flowers by name, may be begun this delightful study. This should be done naturally and informally. The teacher may say: "Thank you, John, for this bouquet. Why, here is a pansy, a bachelor's button, a larkspur and a poppy." Or, "Julia has brought me a beautiful flower. What is its name, I wonder?" Then may follow a little discussion, which the teacher leads to the proper conclusion. If this course is consistently followed, the children will learn the names of the common flowers of wood, field and garden, and never realize that they are learning anything.

The next step is to inspire the child with a desire to care for and preserve his bouquet. The posies brought in the perspiring little hand may be wilted and look dejected; ask their owner to place the stems in water and call attention to the way they lift their drooping heads. Parents and teachers should very early inculcate in children this respect for the rights of flowers which they gather; no matter how tired the child or how disinclined to further effort, when he returns from the woods or fields or garden with plucked flowers, he should be made to place their stems in water immediately. This is a lesson in duty as well as in plant study. Attention to the behavior of the thirsty flowers may be gained by asking the following questions:

1. When a plant is wilted how does it look? How does its stem act? Do its leaves stand up? What happens to the flower?

2. Place the cut end of the stem in water and look at it occasionally during an hour; describe what happens to the stem, the leaves, the blossom.

3. To find how flowers drink, place the stem of a wilted plant in red ink; the next day cut the stem across and find how far the ink has been lifted into it.

Colorado blue columbine aquilegia

How To Make Plants Comfortable

NOTHER step in plant study comes naturally from planting the seeds in window-boxes or garden. This may be done in the kindergarten or in the primary grades. As soon as the children have had some experience in the growing of flowers, they should conduct some experiments which will teach them about the needs of plants. These experiments are fit for the work of the second or third grade. Uncle John says, "All plants want to grow; all they ask is that they shall be made comfortable." The following experiments should be made vital and full of interest, by impressing upon the children that through them they will learn to make their plants comfortable.

EXPERIMENT 1. To find out what kind of soil plants love best to grow in—Have the children of a class, or individuals representing a class, prepare four little pots or boxes, as follows: Fill one with rich, woods humus, or with potting earth from a florist's; another with poor, hard soil, which may be found near excavations; another with clean sand; another with sawdust. Plant the same kind of seeds in all four, and place them where they will get plenty of light. Water them as often as needful. Note which plants grow the best. This trial should cover six weeks at least and attention should now and then be called to the relative growth of the plants.

EXPERIMENT 2. *To prove that plants need light in order to grow.*— Fill two pots with the same rich soil; plant in these the same kind of seeds, and give them both the same amount of water; keep one in the window and place the other in a dark closet or under a box, and note what happens. Or take two potted geraniums which look equally thrifty; keep one in the light and the other in darkness. What happens?

A terrarium. Various plants can be grown, and many kinds of insects, reptiles or amphibians can be perfectly at home in a terrarium that is suitable sized.

EXPERIMENT 3. *To show that the leaves love the light*— Place a geranium in a window and let it remain in the same position for two weeks. Which way do all the leaves face? Turn it around, and note what the leaves have done after a few days.

EXPERIMENT 4. *To show that plants need water*— Fill three pots with rich earth, plant the same kinds of seeds in each, and place them all in the same window. Give one water as it needs it, keep another flooded with water, and give the other none at all. What happens to the seeds in the three pots?

The success of these four experiments depends upon the genius of the teacher. The interest in the result should be keen; every child should feel that every seed planted is a living germ and that it is struggling to grow; every look at the experiments should be like another chapter in a continued story. In the case of young children, I have gone so far as to name the seeds, "Robbie Radish" or "Polly Peppergrass." I did this to focus the attention of the child on the efforts of this living being to grow. After the experiments, the children told the story, personating each seed, thus: "I am Susie Sweet Pea and Johnny Smith planted me in sand. I started to grow, for I had some lunch with me which my mother put up for me to eat when I was hungry; but after

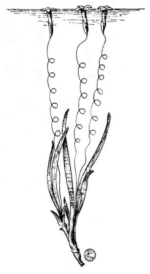

Eel grass, Vallisneria. A quiet-water plant, eel grass produces its male flowers under water, its female flowers bloom at the top. When mature, the male flowers float to the surface, where pollination occurs; the female flowers are then retracted to mature the fruits under water. This plant is the favorite food of canvasback ducks

the lunch was all gone, I could find very little food in the sand, although my little roots reached down and tried and tried to find something for me to eat. I finally grew pale and could not put out another leaf."

The explanations of these experiments should be simple, with no attempt to teach the details of plant physiology. The need of plants for rich, loose earth and for water is easily understood by the children; but the need for light is not so apparent, and Uncle John's story of the starch factory is the most simple and graphic way of making known to the children the processes of plant nourishment. This is how he tells it: "Plants are just like us; they have to have food to make them grow; where is the food and how do they find it? Every green leaf is a factory to make food for the plant; the green pulp in the leaf is the machinery; the leaves get the raw materials from the sap and from the air, and the machinery unites them and makes them into plant food. This is mostly starch, for this is the chief food of plants, although they require some other kinds of food also. The machinery is run by sunshine-power, so the leaf-factory can make nothing without the aid of light; the leaf-factories begin to work as soon as the sun rises, and only stop working when it sets. But the starch has to be changed to sugar before the baby, growing tips of the plant can use it for nourishment and growth; and so the leaves, after making the starch from the sap and the air, are obliged to digest it, changing the starch to sugar; for the growing parts of the plant feed upon sweet sap. Although the starch-factory in the leaves can work only during the daytime, the leaves can change the starch to sugar during the night. So far as we know, there is no starch in the whole world which is not made in the leaf-factories."

Birch trees. Although these birches grow in clumps, several trunks from a common root, observe that the trunks soon separate widely, thus providing abundant light for the leaves

This story should be told and repeated often, until the children realize the work done by leaves for the plants and their need of light.

> "The clouds are at play in the azure space
> And their shadows at play on the bright green vale.
> And here they stretch to the frolic chase;
> And there they roll on the easy gale.
> "There's a dance of leaves in that aspen bower,
> There's a titter of winds in that beechen tree,
> There's a smile on the fruit and a smile on the flower,
> And a laugh from the brook that runs to the sea."
>
> —BRYANT.

How To Teach the Names of the Parts of a Flower and of the Plant

HE scientific names given to the parts of plants have been the stumbling block to many teachers, and yet no part of plant study is more easily accomplished. First of all, the teacher should have in mind clearly the names of the parts which she wishes to teach; the illustrations here given are for her convenience. When talking with the pupils about flowers let her use these names naturally:

"See how many geraniums we have; the corolla of this one is red and of that one is pink. The red corolla has fourteen petals and the pink one only five," etc.

"This arbutus which James brought has a pretty little pink bell for a corolla."

"The purple trillium has a purple corolla, the white trillium a white corolla; and both have green sepals."

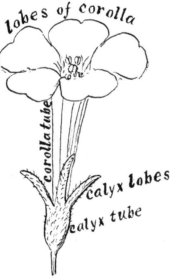

A flower with petals united forming a tube, and with sepals likewise united.

The points to be borne in mind are that children like to call things by their names because they are *real* names, and they also like to use "grown up" names for things; but they do not like to commit to memory names which to them are meaningless. Circumlocution is a waste of breath; calling a petal a "leaf of a flower" or the petiole "the stem of a leaf," is like calling a boy's arm "the projecting part of James' body" or Molly's golden hair "the yellow top" to her head. All the names should be taught gradually by constant unemphasized use on

94

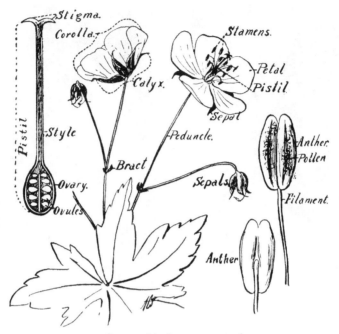

A flower with the parts named

the part of the teacher; and if the child does not learn the names naturally then do not make him do it unnaturally.

The lesson on the garden, or horseshoe geranium with single flowers, is the one to be given first in teaching the structure of a flower since the geranium blossom is simple and easily understood.

A leaf with parts named.

Pomegranate fruit

Teach the Use of the Flower

FROM first to last the children should be taught that the object of the flower is to develop seed. They should look eagerly into the maturing flower for the growing fruit. Poetry is full of the sadness of the fading flower, while rightly it should be the gladness of the flower that fades, because its work is done for the precious seed at its heart. The whole attention of the child should be fixed upon the developing fruit instead of the fading and falling petals.

"In all places then and in all seasons,
Flowers expand their light and soul-like wings,
Teaching us by most persuasive reasons,
How akin they are to human things."

—LONGFELLOW.

Honey bee collecting pollen from a flower. The bee can carry pollen from one flower to another

Flowers and Insect Partners

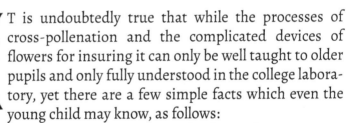

T is undoubtedly true that while the processes of cross-pollenation and the complicated devices of flowers for insuring it can only be well taught to older pupils and only fully understood in the college laboratory, yet there are a few simple facts which even the young child may know, as follows:

1. Pollen is needed to make the seeds grow; some flowers need the pollen from other flowers of the same kind, to make their seeds grow; but many flowers also use the pollen from their own flowers to pollenate their ovules, which grow into seeds.

2. Flowers have neither legs like animals nor wings like butterflies, to go after pollen; so they give insects nectar to drink and pollen to eat, and thus pay them for fetching and carrying the pollen.

I taught this to a four-year-old once in the following manner: A pine tree in the yard was sifting its pollen over us and little Jack asked what the yellow dust was; we went to the tree and saw where it came from, then I found a tiny young cone and explained to him that this was a pine blos-

Butterflies are also great pollinators

som, and that in order to become a cone with seeds, it must have some pollen fall upon it; and we saw how the wind sifted the pollen over it and then we examined a ripe cone and found the seeds. Then we looked at the clovers in the lawn. They did not have so much pollen and they were so low in the grass that the wind could not carry it for them; but right there was a bee. What was she doing? She was getting honey for her hive or pollen for her brood, and she went from one clover head to another; we caught her in a glass fruit jar, and found she was dusted with pollen and that she had pollen packed in the baskets on her hind legs; and we concluded that she carried plenty of pollen on her clothes for the clovers, and that the pollen in her baskets was for her own use. After that he was always watching the bees at work; and we found afterwards that flowers had two ways of telling the insects that they wanted pollen. One was by their color, for the dandelions and clovers hide their colors during dark, rainy days when the bees remain in their hives. Then we found the bees working on mignonette, whose blossoms were so small that Jack did not think they were blossoms at all, and we concluded that the mignonette called the bees by its fragrance. We found other flowers which called with both color and fragrance; and this insect-flower partnership remained a factor of great interest in the child's mind ever after.

Pollen on a bees leg as it visits flowers

"Roly-poly honey-bee,
Humming in the clover,
Under you the tossing leaves,
And the blue sky over,
Why are you so busy, pray?
Never still a minute,
Hovering now above a flower,
Now half buried in it!"

—JULIA C. R. DORR.

The Relation of Plants to Geography

THERE should be from first to last a steady growth in the intelligence of the child as to the places where certain plants grow. He finds hepaticas and trilliums in the woods, daisies and buttercups in the sunny fields, mullein on the dry hillsides, cat-tails in the swamp, and water lilies floating on the pond. This may all be taught by simply asking the pupils questions relating to the soil and the special conditions of the locality where they found the flowers they bring to school.

The plants found in a mountain forest (top) and a rainforest (above) are very different

Newly germinated plants. See the seed shell still stuck to the tips of the original leaves

Seed Germination

Less than three decades ago, this one feature of plant life once came near "gobbling up" all of nature-study, and yet it is merely an incident in the growth of the plant. To sprout seeds is absurd as an object in itself; it is incidental as is the breaking of the egg-shell to the study of the chicken. The peeping into a seed like a bean or a pea, to see that the plant is really there, with its lunch put up by its mother packed all around it, is interesting to the child. To watch the little plant develop, to study its seed-leaves and what becomes of them, to know that they give the plant its first food and to know how a young plant looks and acts, are all items of legitimate interest in the study of the life of a plant; in fact the struggle of the little plant to get free from its seed-coats may be a truly dramatic story. (See "First Lessons with Plants," Bailey, page 79). But to regard this feature as the chief object of planting seed is manifestly absurd.

The object of planting any seed should be to rear a plant which shall fulfill its whole duty and produce other seed. The following observations regarding the germination of seeds should be made while the children are eagerly watching the coming of the plants in their gardens or window-boxes:

1. Which comes out of the seed first, the root or the leaf? Which way does the root always grow, up or down? Which way do the leaves always grow, no matter which side up the seed is planted?

Seeds can be germinated almost anywhere. Here an egg carton has been used

2. How do the seed-leaves try to get out of the seed-coat, or shell? How do the seed-leaves differ in form from the leaves which come later? What becomes of the seed-leaves after the plant begins to grow?

References— First Lessons with Plants, L. H. Bailey; First Lessons in Plant Life, Atkinson; Plants and their Children, Dana; Plants, Coulter; How Plants Grow, Gray; How Plants Behave, Gray.

A hazelnut seedling

A tree showing the effect of prevailing winds from one direction

Tree Study

"I wonder if they like it—being trees?
I suppose they do.
It must feel so good to have the ground so flat,
And feel yourself stand straight up like that.
So stiff in the middle, and then branch at ease,
Big boughs that arch, small ones that bend and blow,
And all those fringy leaves that flutter so.
You'd think they'd break off at the lower end
When the wind fills them, and their great heads bend.
But when you think of all the roots they drop,
As much at bottom as there is on top,
A double tree, widespread in earth and air,
Like a reflection in the water there."
          —"TREE FEELINGS" BY CHARLOTTE PERKINS STETSON.

An avenue of trees

 ATURAL is our love for trees! A tree is a living being, with a life comparable to our own. In one way it differs from us greatly: it is stationary, and it has roots and trunk instead of legs and body; it is obliged to wait to have what it needs come to it, instead of being able to search the wide world over to satisfy its wants.

THE PARTS OF THE TREE

The *head,* or *crown,* is composed of the branches as a whole, which in turn are composed of the larger and smaller branches and twigs. The *spray* is the term given to the outer twigs, the finest divisions of the trunk, which bear the leaves and fruit. The branches are divisions of the *bole,* or *trunk,* which is the body, or stem, of the tree. The bole, at the base, divides into roots, and the roots into rootlets, which are covered with roothairs. It is important to understand what each of the parts of a tree's anatomy does to help carry on the life of the tree.

The roots, which extend out in every direction beneath the surface

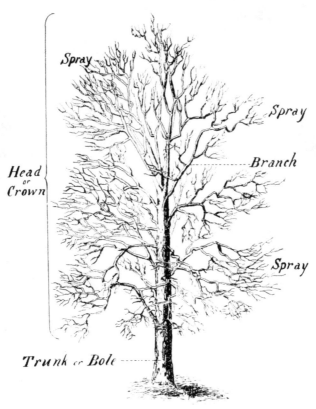

A tree with parts named.

of the ground, have two quite different offices to perform: First, they absorb the water which contains the tree food dissolved from the soil; second, they hold the tree in place against the onslaught of the winds. If we could see a tree standing on its head with its roots spread in the air in the same manner as they are in the ground, we could then better understand that there is as much of the tree hidden below ground as there is in sight above ground, although of quite different shape, being flatter and in a more dense mass. The roots seem to know in which direction to grow to reach water; thus, the larger number of the roots of a tree are often found to extend out toward a stream flowing perhaps some distance from the tree; when they find plenty of food and water the rootlets interlace forming a solid mat. On the Cornell Campus are certain elms which, every six or seven years, completely fill and clog the nearby sewers; these trees send most of their roots in

Annual rings near the center are narrow, but they become much wider.

the direction of the sewer pipe. The fine rootlets upon the tree-roots are covered with root-hairs, which really form the mouths by which the liquid food is taken into the tree.

To understand how firm a base the roots form to hold up the tall trunk, we need to see an uprooted tree. The great roots seem to be molded to take firm grasp upon the soil. It is interesting to study some of the "stump fences" which were made by our forefathers, who uprooted the white pines when the land was cleared of the primeval forest, and made fences of their widespreading but rather shallow extending roots. Many of these fences stand to-day with branching, out-reaching roots, white and weather-worn, but still staunch and massive as if in memory of their strong grasp upon the soil of the wilderness.

The trunk, or bole, or stem of the tree has also two chief offices: It holds the branches aloft, rising to a sufficient height in the forest so that its head shall push through the leaf canopy and expose the leaves to the sunlight. It also is a channel by which the water containing the food surges from root to leaf and back again through each growing part. The branches are divisions of the trunk, and have the same work to do.

Tree roots fighting to hold the riverbank together

In cross-section, the tree trunk shows on the outside the layer of protective bark; next to this comes the cambium layer, which is the vital part of the trunk; it builds on its outside a layer of bark, and on its inside a layer of wood around the trunk. Just within the cambium layer is a lighter colored portion of the trunk, which is called the sap-wood because it is filled with sap which moves up and down its cells in a mysterious manner; the sap-wood consists of the more recent annual rings of growth. Within the sap-wood are concentric rings to the very center or pith; this portion is usually darker in color and is called the heartwood; it no longer has anything to do with the life of the tree, but simply gives to it strength and staunchness. The larger branches, if cut across, show the same structure as the trunk,—the bark on the outside, the cambium layer next, and within this the rings of annual growth. Even the smaller branches and twigs show similar structure, but they are young and have not attained many annual rings.

The leaves are borne on the outermost parts of the tree. A leaf cannot grow, and if it could would be of no use, unless it can be reached by the sunlight. Therefore the trunk lifts the branches aloft, and the branches hold the twigs far out, and the twigs divide into the fine spray, so as to spread the leaves and hold them out into the sunshine.

In structure, the leaf is made up of the stem, or petiole, and the blade, or widened portion of the leaf, which is sustained usually with a framework of many ribs or veins. The petioles and the veins are sap channels like the branches and twigs.

WOOD-GRAIN

This is the way that the sap-river ran

From the root to the top of the tree

Silent and dark,

Under the bark,

Working a wonderful plan

That the leaves never know,

And the branches that grow

On the brink of the tide never see.

—JOHN B. TABB.

THE WAY A TREE GROWS

THE places of growth on a tree may be found at the tips of the twigs and the tips of the rootlets; each year through this growth the tree pushes up higher, down deeper and out farther at the sides. But in addition to all of these growing tips, there is a layer of growth over the entire tree—over every root, over the trunk, over the limbs and over each least twig, just as if a thick coat of paint had been put over the complete tree. It is a coat of growth instead, and these coats of growth make the concentric rings which we see when the trunks or branches are cut across. Such growth as this cannot be made without food; but the tree can take only liquid food from the soil; the root-hairs take up the water in which the "fertilizer" is dissolved, and it is carried up through the larger roots, up through the sap-wood of the trunk, out through the branches to the leaves, where in the leaf-factories the water and free oxygen is given off to the air, and the nourishing elements retained and mixed with certain chemical elements of the air, thus becoming tree food. The leaf is a factory; the green pulp in the leaf cells is part of the machinery; the machinery

Sunlight streaming through pine trees

is set in motion by sunshine power; the raw materials are taken from the air and from the sap containing food from the soil; the finished product is largely starch. Thus, it is well, when we begin the study of the tree, to notice that the leaves are so arranged as to gain all the sunlight possible, for without sunlight the starch factories would be obliged to "shut down." It has been estimated that on a mature maple of vigorous growth there is exposed to the sun nearly a half acre of leaf surface. Our tree appears to us in a new phase when we think of it as a starch factory covering half an acre.

Starch is plant food in a convenient form for storage, and it is stored in sap-wood of the limbs, the branches and trunk, to be used for the growth of the next year's leaves. But starch cannot be assimilated by plants in this form, it must be changed to sugar before it may be used to build up the plant tissues. So the leaves are obliged to perform the office of stomach and digest the food they have made for the tree's use. In the mysterious laboratory of the leaf-cells, the starch is changed to sugar; and nitrogen, sulphur, phosphorus and other substances are taken from the sap and starch added to them, and thus are

Trees in winter

made the proteids which form another part of the tree's diet. It is interesting to note that while the starch factories can operate only in the sunlight, the leaves can digest the food and it can be transported and used in the growing tissues in the *dark*. The leaves are also an aid to the tree in breathing, but they are not especially the lungs of the tree. The tree breathes in certain respects as we do; it takes in oxygen and gives off carbon dioxide; but the air containing the oxygen is taken in through the numerous pores in the leaves called stomata, and also through lenticels in the bark; so the tree really breathes all over its active surface.

The tree is a rapid worker and achieves most of its growth and does most of its work by midsummer. The autumn leaf which is so beautiful has completed its work. The green starch-machinery or chlorophyl, the living protoplasm in the leaf cells, has been withdrawn and is safely secluded in the woody part of the tree. The autumn leaf which glows gold or red, has in it only the material which the tree can no longer use. It is a mistake to believe that the frost causes the brilliant colors of autumn foliage; they are caused by the natural old age and death of the leaves—and where is there to be found old age and death more beautiful? When the leaf assumes its bright colors, it is making ready to depart from the tree; a thin, corky layer is being developed between its petiole and the twig, and when this is perfected, the leaf drops from its own weight or the touch of the slightest breeze.

A tree, growing in open ground, records in its shape, the direction of the prevailing winds. It grows more luxuriantly on the leeward side. It touches the heart of the one who loves trees to note their sturdy endurance of the onslaughts of this, their most ancient enemy.

Reference Books for Tree Study— The Tree Book, Julia Rogers; *Our Native Trees*, Harriet Keeler; *Our Northern Shrubs*, Harriet Keeler; *The Trees of the Northern States*, Romayne Hough. *The Trees*, N. L. Britton; *Getting Acquainted with the Trees*, J. Horace McFarland; *Familiar Trees and their Leaves*, Schuyler Mathews; *Our Trees and How to Know Them*, Clarence Moores Weed; *A Guide to the Trees*, Alice Lounsberry; *The First Book of Forestry*, Filibert Roth; *Practical Forestry*, John Gifford; *Trees in Prose and Poetry*, Stone & Fickett; *The Primers of Forestry*, Pinchot.

As the elevation increases the trees become stunted near the timberline

Acorns

How To Begin Tree Study

URING autumn the attention of the children should be attracted to the leaves by their gorgeous colors. It is well to use this interest to cultivate their knowledge of the forms of leaves of trees; but the teaching of the tree species to the young child should be done quite incidentally and guardedly. If the teacher says to the child bringing a leaf, "This is a white oak leaf," the child will soon quite unconsciously learn that leaf by name. Thus, tree study may be begun in the kindergarten or the primary grades.

1. Let the pupils use their leaves as a color lesson by classifying them according to color, and thus train the eye to discriminate tints and color values.

2. Let them classify the leaves according to form, selecting those which resemble each other.

3. Let each child select a leaf of his own choosing and draw it. This may be done by placing the leaf flat on paper and outlining it with pencil or with colored crayon.

4. Let the pupils select paper of a color similar to the chosen leaf and cut a paper leaf like it.

5. Let each pupil select four leaves which are similar and arrange them on a card in a symmetrical design. This may be done while the leaves are fresh, and the card with leaves may be pressed and thus preserved.

Oak leaves

In the fourth grade, begin with the study of a tree which grows near the schoolhouse. In selecting this tree and in speaking of it, impress upon the children that it is a living being, with a life and with needs of its own. I believe so much in making this tree seem an individual, that I would if necessary name it Pocahontas or Martha Washington. First, try to ascertain the age of the tree. Tell an interesting story of who planted it and who were children and attended school in the schoolhouse when the tree was planted. To begin the pupils' work, let each have a little note-book in which shall be written, sketched or described all that happens to this particular tree for a year. The following words with their meaning should be given in the reading and spelling lessons: *Head, bole, trunk, branches, twigs, spray, roots, bark, leaf, petiole, foliage, sap.*

LESSON

Fall (Autumn) Work—

1. What is the color of the tree in its autumn foliage? Sketch it in water colors or crayons, showing the shape of the head, the relative proportions of head and trunk.

2. Describe what you can see of the tree's roots. How far do you suppose the roots reach down? How far out at the sides? In how many ways are the roots useful to the tree? Do you suppose, if the tree were turned bottomside up, that it would show as many roots as it now shows branches?

Fall colors

3. How high on the trunk from the ground do the lower branches come off? How large around is the trunk three feet from the ground? If you know how large around it is, how can you get the distance through? What is the color of the bark? Is the bark smooth or rough? Are the ridges fine or coarse? Are the furrows between the ridges deep or shallow? Of what use is the bark to the tree?

4. Describe the leaf from your tree, paying special attention to its shape, its edges, its color above and below, its veins or ribs, and the relative length and thickness of its petiole. Are the leaves set opposite or alternate upon the twigs? As the leaves begin to fall, can you find two which are exactly the same in size and shape? Draw in your note-book the two leaves which differ most from each other of any that grew on your tree. At what date do the leaves begin to fall from your tree? At what date are they all off the tree?

5. Do you find any fruit or seed upon your tree? If so describe and sketch it, and tell how you think it is scattered and planted.

Winter Study of the Tree—

1. Make a sketch of the tree in your notebook, showing its shape as it stands bare. Does the trunk divide into branches, or does it extend through the center of the tree and the branches come off from its

Trees in winter

sides? Of what use are the branches to a tree? Is the spray, or the twigs at the end of the branches, coarse or fine? Does it lift up or droop? Is the bark on the branches like that on the trunk? Is the color of the spray the same as of the large branches? Why does the tree drop its leaves in winter? Does the tree grow during the winter? Do you think that it sleeps during the winter?

2. Study the cut end of a log or stump and also study a slab. Which is the heart-wood and which is the sap-wood? Can you see the rings of growth? Can you count these rings and tell how old was the tree from which this log came? Describe if you can, how a tree trunk grows larger each year. What is it makes the grain in the wood which we use for furniture? If we girdle a tree why does it die? If we place a nail in a tree three feet from the ground this winter, will it be any higher from the ground ten years from now? How does the tree grow tall?

3. Take a twig of a tree in February and look carefully at the buds. What is their color? Are they shiny, rough, sticky or downy? Are they arranged on the twigs opposite or alternate? Can you see the scar below the buds where the last year's leaf was borne? Place the twig in water and put in a light, warm place, and see what happens to the buds. As the leaves push out, what happens to the scales which protected the buds?

Spring

4. What birds do you find visiting your tree during winter? Tie some strips of beef fat upon its branches, and note all of the kinds of birds which come to feast upon it.

Spring Work—

1. At what date do the young leaves appear upon your tree? What color are they? Look carefully to see how each leaf was folded in the bud. Were all the leaves folded in the same way? Are the young leaves thin, downy and tender? Do they stand out straight as did the old leaves last autumn, or do they droop? Why? Will they change position and stand out as they grow stronger? Why do the leaves stand out from the twigs in order to get sunshine? What would happen to a tree if it lost all its leaves in spring and summer? Tell all of the things you know which the leaves do for the tree.

2. Are there any blossoms on your tree in the spring? If so, how do they look? Are the blossoms which bear the fruit on different trees from those that bear the pollen, or are these flowers placed separately on the same tree? Or does the same flower which produces the pollen also produce the seed? Do the insects carry the pollen from flower to flower, or does the wind do this for your tree? What sort of seeds are formed by these flowers? How are the seeds scattered and planted?

Young leaves and blossoms emerge from buds in spring

3. At what date does your tree stand in full leaf? What color is it now? What birds do you find visiting it? What insects? What animals seek its shade? Do the squirrels live in it?

4. Measure the height of your tree as follows: Choose a bright, sunny morning for this. Take a stick 3 ½ feet long and thrust it in the ground so that three feet will project above the soil. Immediately measure the length of its shadow and of the shadow which your tree makes from its base to the shadow of its topmost twigs. Supposing that the shadow from the stick is 4 feet long and the shadow from your tree is 80 feet long, then your example will be: 4 ft. : 3 ft. :: 80 ft. : ? which will make the tree 60 feet high.

To measure the circumference of the tree, take the trunk three feet from the ground and measure it exactly with a tape measure. To find the thickness of the trunk, divide the circumference just found by 3.14.

Supplementary Reading—Among Green Trees, Rogers; Chap. I in A Primer of Forestry, Pinchot; Part I in A First Book of Forestry, Roth; Chapter IV in Practical Forestry, Gifford.

How To Make Leaf Prints

A very practical help in interesting children in trees, is to encourage them to make portfolios of leaf-prints of all the trees of the region. Although the process is mechanical, yet the fact that every print must be correctly labeled makes for useful knowledge. One of my treasured possessions is such a portfolio made by the lads of St. Andrews School of Richmond, Va., who were guided and inspired in this work by their teacher, Professor W. W. Gillette. The impressions were made in green ink and the results are as beautiful as works of art. Professor Gillette gave me my first lesson in making leaf prints.

Material—

1. A smooth slate, or better, a thick plate of glass, about 12 x 15 inches.

2. A tube of printer's ink, either green or black, and costing 50 cents; one tube contains a sufficient supply of ink for making several hundred prints. Or a small quantity of printer's ink may be purchased at any printing office.

3. Two six-inch rubber rollers, such as photographers use in mounting prints, which cost 15 cents each. A letter-press may be used instead of one roller.

4. A small bottle of kerosene to dilute the ink, and a bottle of benzine for cleaning the outfit after using, care being taken to store them safe from fire.

5. Sheets of paper 8 ½ x 11 inches. The paper should be of good quality, with smooth surface in order that it may take and hold a clear outline. The ordinary paper used in printers' offices for printing newspapers works fairly well. I have used with success the paper from blank notebooks which cost five cents a piece.

To make a print, place a few drops of ink upon the glass or slate, and spread it about with the roller until there is a thin coat of ink upon the roller and a smooth patch in the center of the glass or slate. It should never be so liquid as to "run," for then the outlines will be blurred.

Nika Akin

Leaf print of a sycamore maple

Ink the leaf by placing it on the inky surface of the glass and passing the inked roller over it once or twice until the veins show that they are smoothly filled. Now place the inked leaf between two sheets of paper and roll *once* with the *clean* roller, bearing on with all the strength possible; a second passage of the roller blurs the print.

Two prints are made at each rolling, one of the upper, and one of the under side of the leaf. Dry and wrinkled leaves may be made pliant by soaking in water, drying between blotters before they are inked.

Prints may also be made a number at a time by pressing them under weights, being careful to put the sheets of paper with the leaves between the pages of old magazines or folded newspapers, in order that the impression of one set of leaves may not mar the others. If a letter-press is available for this purpose, it does the work quickly and well.

SAP

Strong as the sea and silent as the grave,
It flows and ebbs unseen,
Flooding the earth, a fragrant tidal wave,
With mists of deepening green.

—JOHN B. TABB.

CPSIA information can be obtained
at www.ICGtesting.com
Printed in the USA
LVHW081002030321
680374LV00066B/1091

9 781922 348746